THE PORT OF LONDON AUTHORITY
A CENTURY OF SERVICE
1909-2009

THE PORT OF LONDON AUTHORITY
A CENTURY OF SERVICE
1909-2009

Nigel Watson

© Nigel Watson & The Port of London Authority, 2009

ISBN-10   0-9543782-6-1
ISBN-13   978-0-9543782-6-4

Published by St Matthew's Press
For the Port of London Authority
London River House
Royal Pier Road
Gravesend, Kent DA12 2BG
United Kingdom

Design and artwork by Brian Glanfield CREATIVE DESIGN

Printed and bound by
Butler Tanner & Dennis Ltd, Caxton Road, Frome, Somerset BA11 1NF
United Kingdom

Contents

FOREWORD BY SIMON SHERRARD, CHAIRMAN, THE PORT OF LONDON AUTHORITY

Organisations reaching their centenary are few in number. The Port of London Authority has achieved this milestone playing its part throughout a hundred years of change on the River Thames, to the benefit of the nation's capital and the country as a whole.

To have produced a history covering in detail the many diverse influences that have shaped the port activities on the river since 1909 would have resulted in a tome, the thickness of which would have daunted even the most avid student of twentieth-century London. We have therefore sought to publish a book identifying the key issues that have been faced, how they were addressed and how they have shaped the Port of London of today and indeed the Authority as it continues its vital services into the current century.

The challenges encountered over the decades have been substantial. The PLA was created to resolve the chaos resulting from the myriad of competing terminals in a much less regulated era and the detrimental effect this was having on London and river safety and ecology. We have had to address the progressive move of port activities downriver as ships became bigger and cargo handling methods changed as well as the impact this had on the working population. Ultimately, after more than eighty years we ceased being a terminal operator with the privatisation of Tilbury. Since then we have focused on the core responsibility that has run throughout our existence – being regulator of the river.

As we enter our next century prospects for trade in the Port look most encouraging. Demonstrating the robustness of the organisational model conceived one hundred years ago as it has evolved, we are today ensuring that new developments, such as DP World's London Gateway Port with its much larger ships, can be assimilated into the river without inconvenience to other river users and without compromising the already high standards of navigational safety in the Port.

While the PLA was founded to address what was essentially a cargo related problem our remit today extends beyond this to encompass all river users whether their objective is sporting, leisure or to provide essential services to passengers or tourists. All users benefit from our key objectives: to keep the river safe, to protect the marine environment and to ensure that this great national asset continues to play its part in the prosperity of the country.

For me, the PLA's centenary falls as I complete nine years as Chairman. It has been a privilege to serve this organisation containing as it does people of immense skill and commitment, continuing a tradition that has been a hallmark of the Authority since its beginnings. I have no doubt that the vital role that the PLA plays will be equally appreciated and relevant one hundred years from now.

Simon Sherrard
Chairman, Port of London Authority
December 2008

Notes on Measurements and Monetary Values.

Weight - Throughout the text the usage of the imperial ton or the metric tonne is dependent on which term was in use at the time. The appendix on cargo tonnages has been converted into tonnes.

Area – The same rule has been applied in relation to acreage. For those wishing to convert acres into hectares, the former should be multiplied by 0.405.

Distance – Miles are still commonly used in the United Kingdom and this measurement is used throughout the text.

Depth and Length – Metric measurements to the nearest metre are given alongside imperial measurements.

Monetary Values – To assist the reader, many of these are followed in brackets by current values.

ACKNOWLEDGEMENTS

This book is an introduction to the Port of London Authority. In celebrating the PLA's centenary, it takes a glimpse at its past, briefly describes the Authority today and sums up the aspirations of the Authority for the future. It is no substitute for the history of this remarkable institution that remains to be written.

Many people have contributed towards this book. The PLA documentary archive is in the care of Claire Frankland, Archivist (Port & River), Museum in Docklands and its images in the care of Anna Sparham, Curator, Images – Museum of London. This book could not have been completed without their friendly help and advice.

Chris Ellmers, whose immense knowledge of the Authority and its work is almost unrivalled, kindly reviewed the text, offered counsel and wrote many of the brief 'insets' that help bring the story to life.

A number of people kindly spoke to me about the PLA past and present and I am grateful to Bob Aspinall, Bill Bean, John Carr, David Cartlidge, Fraser Clift, Gordon Dickins, Keith Doggett, Geoff Ennals, Richard Everitt, Ian Flanders, Alistair Gale, David Jeffery, Jeff Jenkinson, Sally Mashiter, Martin Round, Simon Sherrard, Sir Brian Shaw and Cyril Webb.

The text has been immeasurably improved thanks to guidance and comments from several people, and I would particularly like to thank Alan Cartwright, Robert Baldwin, Chris Ellmers and Alistair Gale. Jim Trimmer and Jeremy Smith also deserve special mention for prompt, thorough and thoughtful reviews of drafts.

Finally, I must say thank you to Samantha Broome at the PLA for all her invaluable help in arranging interviews and administering the project.

Nigel Watson
December 2008

This very accurate watercolour view of the West India Docks in 1814 was commissioned from George Underwood by Sir John Soane for use in his public lectures.
(Courtesy of the Sir John Soane Museum)

1

BEFORE THE PORT OF LONDON AUTHORITY

For the last hundred years the Port of London Authority has been the custodian of the tidal Thames and the Port it supports. Today its jurisdiction runs along 95 miles (150 kilometres) of the river from Teddington Lock to the outer Thames estuary, up to a line lying roughly between Margate and Clacton. The lasting impact of the Authority is undeniable. Familiar for generations to many Londoners as the PLA, the Authority has succeeded where its predecessors failed. When the Port's reputation was under threat, the creation of the PLA helped to sustain it. After the terrible destruction suffered by the Port during the Second World War, the PLA helped to rebuild it. When there seemed to be little hope for the Port, as the conventional docks closed under the pressure of radical changes in the way cargo was handled, the PLA gave it a future by investing in a modern container terminal. Under the Authority's watchful eye, the Thames has become safer and cleaner. It has reconciled the diverse ways in which the tidal Thames is used, from athletic rowers in their fours and eights and occasional sailors taking to the water at the weekends to pleasure-boat operators carrying countless tourists and shipping companies sending container vessels into Tilbury and supertankers to Coryton. Thousands of years after the first cargo was brought ashore from the river, the PLA has helped to ensure that the Thames remains a working river and an essential part of the trading fabric of the nation.

How did it all begin? One of the most famous rivers in the world gave birth to one of its greatest cities. Together they spawned one of its most powerful empires, transforming London into the world's greatest port. For centuries, the river almost seemed to manage itself, but imperial expansion, growth in trade, bigger ships and an increasing population all took their toll by the middle of the nineteenth century. It was half a century before the resulting turmoil was sorted out and most of the competing parties at last agreed a new organisation should be formed to bring some order to the chaos.

The West India Dock on the Isle of Dogs, opened by William Pitt, the Prime Minister, in 1802, was the first of the docks on the north bank of the river. It was the outcome of a long campaign begun in the 1790s. This had been conducted largely by the West India merchants whose trade in the port had overtaken in value that of the East Indies. The dock was sanctioned in an Act for Rendering more Commodious and for Better Regulating the Port of London in 1799, which, as the title suggests, also intended to provide some relief from growing congestion.

St Katharine Dock was opened in 1828 and operated until closure in 1968.

Although the West India Dock Act gave the dock company a 21-year monopoly on West Indian trade, it also exempted bargemen and lightermen from paying dock dues, through the so-called 'free water' clause, as long as they delivered or received cargoes to and from ships. The consequence was the frequent transhipment of cargoes to and from the wharves along the river. The same clause was obligatory for the other new docks opened over the next few years – London Dock (1805), East India Dock (1806) and St Katharine Dock (1828). It was also applied to the bigger docks built on the north side of the river to handle the new and larger steamships – Victoria Dock (1855), Millwall Dock (1868), South West India Dock (1870), Royal Albert Dock (1880) and Tilbury Dock (1886). On the south bank, the only docks were the Surrey Commercial Docks, specialising in grain, foodstuffs and timber, which had developed piecemeal during the early 1800s from a late-seventeenth-century wet dock.

Despite this progress, the world's greatest port was in administrative and commercial disarray by the end of the nineteenth century. Most of the private dock companies, engaged in fierce competition, were often at war with each other. Weakened financially by undercutting each other's rates, they were prohibited from charging full dues to the bargemen and lightermen who crowded their docks. In competition with the private wharves along the river, many of them were making insufficient profit for the investment needed to maintain the Port's leading international position. Ship-owners began to lose their faith in the docks as the service they provided became more unreliable.

In spite of such problems, there still remained a remarkable confidence within the Port. This had been evident in the engineering triumph achieved by the London & St Katharine Docks Company in the Royal Docks. It was an infectious confidence which had inspired their rivals, the East & West India Dock Company, to develop Tilbury Dock further downstream. This was equally advanced in engineering terms, and similarly endowed with integrated rail links, even if the Company could scarcely afford to finance it. For a long time Tilbury seemed to many to be isolated from the rest of the docks, to be developing in a contrary direction, and to be under-performing. Yet decades hence the ultimate survival of the Port would depend upon Tilbury and the different approach that applied there.

Tilbury's reputation perhaps stemmed from its unhappy beginnings. Opened in 1886, the new dock initially attracted so little business that the East & West India Dock Company was forced to cut rates to ridiculous

A birds-eye view of Tilbury Docks in the year of their opening, 1886. With little warehousing, goods were transported to London by barges and trains.

Tall, funnelled paddle steamers and sailing ships in the
Port of London, showing the congestion on the river.
1840, by William Parrott.

The call-on at London Dock in 1902,
with dockers queueing up for work.

levels. This obliged its rival, the London & St Katharine
Docks Company, to follow suit. In 1888 the prospect of
financial ruin led both managements to reach an agreement to run their operations jointly and they formed a
Joint Docks Committee which took over the majority of
the docks in January 1889.

This was the year of the famous strike by
dockworkers over the 'dockers' tanner'. As well as winning
an extra penny an hour, the strike also won recognition for
the dockers' union. It was this influence which resulted
in the Joint Dock Committee introducing a system of

permanent and registered labourers. This was intended to ameliorate the persistent problem of casual labour within the docks and limit the power of the unions. Men were called on and called off according to fluctuating demand; when there was no work, they were not paid. With a surplus of men, employers had the upper hand. The call-on became a demeaning sight, with foremen picking and choosing from the hundreds of men who would gather early every morning at the dock gates. Ship-owners, used to employing stevedores on contract to load their ships, encouraged this casual labour. With too many men chasing too little work, many of them earning minimal wages while working in often appalling conditions, this system plagued London, as well as other ports, for decades. Finding a solution would tax the minds of

workers, trades unionists, management and government for a hundred years. Many of those attempting to resolve the problem would turn to the scheme introduced by the Joint Dock Committee as a basis for improvements.

The 1880s and 1890s were difficult economic times for the Port, revealing how inextricably its fortunes were linked with the wider world. A decline in trade with India was followed by severe droughts in Australia, resulting in the curtailment of shipments of wool. All this increased the problems facing the dock companies. The Joint Dock Committee was by far the largest dock operator, running not only London Dock, St Katharine Dock, East India Dock, West India Dock and Tilbury, but also the Royal Victoria and Royal Albert Docks. Yet it was barely profitable. As well as the general economic downturn, the

South West India Dock in 1900, with a forest of masts rather than funnels, and lightermen under oars in the middle of the dock.

Joint Dock Committee was also suffering from the effects of the 'free water' clause and competition from riverside wharfingers, who handled by far the larger share of warehousing trade in the Port. In 1901 all these pressures compelled the two companies to amalgamate as the London & India Docks Company.

The remaining dock operations, the Rotherhithe docks run by the Surrey Commercial Dock Company and the Millwall Dock run by the Millwall Freehold Land &

Dock Company, were more successful. The Surrey Docks in particular had flourished through the importation of timber to meet the needs of the expanding capital. Since timber could be floated in the array of ponds within the docks until it was needed, the Surrey Docks also suffered much less from the 'free water' clause. It was a profitable, professional and proud organisation.

By 1900 the Port of London was a paradox – although it was the leading port in the world, its management was a shambles. The London County Council (LCC) had been pressing for reform since 1888, urging the creation of a municipal port authority. The London Chamber of Commerce summed up the general complaints about the port – charges were too high, delivery was too slow, lighterage was poor, rail links were inadequate, there were delays in berthing and unloading, and shipping channels were too shallow. As there was no single authority for the Port, these problems were not easily resolved – the competing dock companies ran the docks; Trinity House was responsible for river pilots; the Watermen's Company licensed the watermen and lightermen; the Corporation of London acted as the sanitary authority; policing was in the hands of the Metropolitan Police, the Kent and Essex constabularies and the dock companies' own police forces; and the Thames Conservancy was the conservation and navigation authority.

The Conservancy had replaced the Navigation Committee of the Corporation of the City of London in 1857. With responsibility for the whole of the river, from the headwaters at Cricklade out into the estuary, the Conservancy initially worked hard to improve the river, removing shoals, upgrading piers, moorings and landings, and regulating traffic. Partly because of financial constraints, the Conservancy was slow in responding to pressure for widening the channel upstream from Gravesend to take the bigger ships coming up the Thames. Work began in 1896 but by 1900 the main channel, instead of being at least the required 30 feet (9 metres) deep, ranged in depth from just 18 feet (5 metres) at Millwall to 26 feet (8 metres) at Gravesend. In 1906 the Conservators finally received parliamentary approval to borrow funds for further dredging. By late 1908 a channel 30 feet (9 metres) deep and 1,000 feet (300 metres) wide had been dredged from Sea Reach to Tilbury.

By 1900 the dock compa-

nies in London were so desperate that they tried to abolish the 'free water' clause by promoting a private Bill in Parliament. This outraged the lightermen and wharfingers and the resulting furore at last stirred the government into action. A Royal Commission was announced, 'To inquire into the present administration of the Port and the water approaches thereto … and to report whether any change or improvement … is necessary for the promotion of the trade of the Port and in the public interest'. The Commission sat during 1900, with 114 witnesses giving evidence over 31 days. Sir Joseph Broodbank, secretary of the London & India Docks Company, and later one of the first members of the new port authority, summarised the evidence as 'a series of attacks upon the existing order of things, and the defence of those responsible for the administration of the Port'. Much of the evidence given to the Commission revolved around how London could maintain its leading position as Continental ports expanded rapidly. Broodbank also noted the Commis-

Millwall Docks in 1895 - an etching by Walter Sarfras.

sion's belief that the docks were as essential for the operation of the Port as the river itself. The Commission, he wrote, concluded that 'these two closely connected elements of the Port should no longer be controlled by independent authorities'.

In 1902 the report of the Commission recommended a unified Port Authority to carry out the necessary investment for the modernisation of the Port and the improvement of the river. It proposed that the powers of the Thames Conservancy, Trinity House and the Watermen's & Lightermen's Company should be transferred to the new Authority. But the Commission rejected the idea

that the Authority should also have responsibility for river buoys and lights, health or river policing. The Authority would have jurisdiction over the length of the tidal Thames, from Teddington Lock downstream to a line drawn between Havengore Creek in Essex and Warden Point on the Isle of Sheppey in Kent. The Conservancy would continue to manage the river upstream from Teddington Lock. The Commission also proposed that the Authority should take over the dock companies, financed by issuing redeemable Port Stock. Interest on the Stock, and the running costs of the Authority, would be funded by charging Port rates on most vessels using the river and levying dues on every vessel entering the docks.

The Conservative government, divided over the future of trade with the Empire, proved too weak to stand

Fishing boats in the Pool of London,
a watercolour by T B Hardy, 1890.

up to continued protests from vested interests and the first Bill was abandoned in 1903. As the recommendations of the Royal Commission gathered dust, so the situation in the Port grew worse, with the uncertainty causing the dock companies to put off any further investment. It was only in 1906, four years after the Commission had reported, when a reforming Liberal government was elected with a huge majority, that the report was dusted off by the new President of the Board of Trade, David Lloyd George, one of the rising talents of the Liberal party. His method of privately negotiating legislation before it was brought to the House of Commons, by consulting widely with interested parties, removing obstacles, and winning over determined opponents (the ship-owners were astonished to be asked for their views), proved

critical in pushing through change. He won over the prosperous Surrey Commercial Docks, the only company in any position to negotiate terms, by offering them a premium by comparison with the valuation of the other dock companies. Lloyd George was also acutely aware of encouraging petroleum supplies to meet rising demand in and around the capital and ensured the new Authority was given the powers to regulate the petroleum trade on the river. This was a crucial step for the future prosperity of both the Port and the Authority.

The challenge of negotiating with the dock companies was taken up by Lloyd George's parliamentary secretary, Hudson Kearley, a successful businessman. He proved so effective that he later became the first chairman of the new port authority as Sir Hudson Kearley, ultimately

A Belgian steamer discharging her cargo
below London Bridge in 1905.

Watermen with their skiffs on the Thames around 1890.
They were vital for the movement of passengers and goods

better known as Lord Devonport, from the title conferred on him in 1910. The Bill was introduced by Lloyd George in April 1908, although within a fortnight he had been appointed Chancellor of the Exchequer. The challenge of guiding the Bill through the House fell to his successor, Winston Churchill. With the Conservative party also committed to reform, the Bill received Royal Assent as the Port of London Act, 1908, on 21 December 1908.

The new Port of London Authority (PLA) was a self-governing public trust and followed the pattern set by the Mersey Docks & Harbour Board in 1858. The powers granted to the Authority mirrored almost exactly the recommendations of the Royal Commission. One major exception was that marine pilots, operating in the English Channel and the Thames, remained under the supervision of Trinity House – until 1988 when they too became part of the PLA. The Authority also acquired the river bed previously owned by the Thames Conservancy, with a percentage of the income from it paid to the Crown.

Lloyd George later described the Authority as representing 'the spirit of compromise, which is the characteristic of our people, something which represents no clear principle of any sort or kind, but which is outside every principle you can lay down and yet works'. In the nature of compromise, the new Authority had strengths and weaknesses. One of its strengths was that it brought together the vested interests in the Port – 18 of the 28 members were elected by those paying port rates, wharfingers and owners of river craft, while the remaining ten were appointed by the Admiralty, the Board of Trade, LCC, the City of London Corporation and Trinity House. In recognition of labour's importance within the partnership of interests in the Port, there were places for trades unionists through the appointments made by the Board of Trade and LCC. This broad representation,

To be effective, the new Authority required strong leadership. So it was that on 3 March 1909 Hudson Kearley was appointed the PLA's first chairman. The Authority met for the first time in the former offices of the London & India Dock Company, at 109, Leadenhall Street, on 16 March. In his inaugural address the Chairman rehearsed the powers and responsibilities of the PLA and acknowledged London's history and traditions as well as its status as the world's leading port. He recognised the central role of the Authority and the importance of relationships with other parties within the Port. 'These powers,' he said, 'are intended to afford permanent benefit to the trade and commerce of the Port; but if unwisely or imprudently exercised they might easily prove a burdensome task, and so injure its growth and expansion. … it will be our determination, I am certain, so to discharge our duties that every interest may derive benefit from our administration and the Port Authority will gain in public esteem and confidence in proportion as it makes this apparent.' He was confident that if the Authority was successful, then:

combined with the Authority's responsibility for the navigation of the tidal Thames and the operation of all the docks, excepting Regent's Canal Dock and Brentford Dock, at last made it possible for future improvements to the Port to be planned centrally.

Among the weaknesses of the new arrangement was the perpetuation of the 'free water' clause. The Authority, through its ownership and operation of the enclosed docks, was a major commercial force in the Port. Yet the wharfingers, the PLA's direct commercial rivals, by their representation on the Board, were privy to all the PLA's decisions. Sometimes it was difficult for the wharfingers – and others on the Board, including the shipping companies and union representatives – to decide whether they had a higher duty to the Authority or to their own interests. The Act gave the Authority the power to buy the riverside wharves but this was not exercised until the purchase of Denton Wharf, bought in 1990 as the principal base for the PLA's fleet and Marine Services operation.

'the benefit will not be for the London of today and tomorrow, but we shall have laid the foundations of an enduring prosperity that will extend far into and enrich the future.'

On 31 March the Authority took over the assets of the dock companies for the sum of £23 million (approximately £1700 million today). This was not greeted with universal rejoicing. At the offices of the profitable Surrey Commercial Docks, the outgoing board of directors flew the company flag at half-mast.

An artist's impression of the King George V Dock
by Charles de Lacy printed in the 1921
commemorative opening booklet.

2 THE PORT OF LONDON AUTHORITY 1909–1992

1909–1921

In little more than a decade, the PLA made its mark upon the Port. Under the dynamic leadership of Lord Devonport, the Authority invested heavily in modernising and extending the docks and improving the river. Although none of this prevented London losing its position as the world's leading port before 1914, and the war delayed the completion of several projects, the Authority's self-confidence in the future was signalled by the opening of the King George V Dock in 1921.

From a standing start, the PLA achieved a huge amount in the years before the First World War. This owed much to the character of the first Chairman, Lord Devonport. Brusque, energetic and assertive, ambitious, self-opinionated and wilful, he was in his element at the PLA, where he remained until 1925. He had to create an organisation from scratch, uniting thousands of employees once divided between several different employers, while pressing ahead with urgent investment in the Port. As a self-financing public trust, set up along the lines of the civil service, with an over-large Board and government by committee, the PLA needed an energetic Chairman to drive the new organisation forward. Whatever his faults, Devonport certainly did that.

He overshadowed the earliest General Managers. He quickly became impatient with the first, Robert Philipson, previously Secretary of the Thames Conservancy. He was irritated by Philipson's attachment to what Devonport considered to be the hide-bound practices of the previous authorities. Philipson's position was also weakened by his collusion with a Board member in several instances of nepotism. In 1913 Devonport forced the retirement of Philipson and the resignation of the member concerned. Philipson's successor, Cumberland Lowndes, formerly

Assistant Chief Goods Manager of the London & North Western Railway, lasted just three years. Between 1916 and the appointment of David Owen as General Manager in 1922, Devonport divided the day-to-day management of the PLA between four divisional officers, the Chief Engineer, the Docks and Warehouses Manager, the Chief Police Officer and the Secretary, who also had responsibility for the River Department.

The PLA's Chief Engineers were central to the development and implementation of Devonport's vision for the Port. The first was Frederick, later Sir Frederick, Palmer, formerly Chief Engineer of the Port of Calcutta. He submitted his plans for the Port to the PLA Board at the end of 1910. Palmer estimated the cost of his ambitious three-phase development programme at £14.5 million, more than a thousand million pounds today. The priority was to remedy at least a decade of under-investment and equip the Port for the future. Significant works were begun during 1911–13, comprising the widening of dock entrances and quays, the construction of new sheds, and various dock extensions. Palmer was succeeded in 1913 by Cyril, later Sir Cyril, Kirkpatrick, who oversaw the continuing development of the docks until his departure in 1924.

Cargo discharged from lighters being tallied by uniformed PLA staff as well as shipping clerks on the quayside at the London Docks around 1905.

HUDSON KEARLEY, 1ˢᵀ VISCOUNT DEVONPORT (1856–1934), FIRST CHAIRMAN OF THE PLA, 1909–1925

Hudson Kearley, Viscount Devonport, the resolute and decisive first Chairman of the PLA (1909-1925) and a key figure in its early development.

The son of a plumber, Hudson Ewbanke Kearley, to give him his full name, began work for the tea firm, Tetley's, at the age of 16, founded his own wholesaling business at the age of 20 and opened his first shop aged 22. By 1890, there were 200 branches of International Stores, as the chain was called.

He entered the House of Commons in 1892. In 1906 he became parliamentary secretary to the Board of Trade under Lloyd George, which proved to be the entrance to his eventual post with the PLA.

His character comes through in a story told by L M Bates. Devonport was negotiating to buy some carpets from the PLA's Cutler Street Warehouses and summoned an Armenian Jewish carpet merchant to his office. Devonport's angry voice could be heard, accompanied by much desk thumping, and eventually the shaken owner emerged to say a deal had been done but he was unsure whether Devonport was to pay him or he was to pay Devonport.

He was a shrewd Chairman. In 1917, when the Board of Trade refused to allow the PLA to raise port charges, Devonport persuaded every member of his Board to sign a joint letter of resignation, successfully calling the Board of Trade's bluff. In the same year, however, his political ambitions had effectively ended after an ineffective period as food controller, despite his experience both as a food retailer and Chairman of the largest Port Authority in the country. Nevertheless, none of his weaknesses should overshadow his considerable achievements at the PLA.

A striking portrayal of the grain elevators in the Surrey Commercial Docks, an oil painting by Dora Meeson dating from 1912.

Investment also poured into the river as work began on deepening channels to take larger ships, with nine dredgers in constant operation, and a fleet of 21 steam hoppers taking dredged material out to sea for disposal. Between 1909 and 1914 the river bed was cleared of 46 wrecks. Another important early achievement on the river had been accomplished on 1 January 1913. Under the Port of London Act, 1912, the Authority paid a lump sum to the Crown to buy out its interest in a percentage of the income the PLA received from the river bed transferred by the Crown in the 1850s.

The investment made by the Authority helped it to reap the benefits of flourishing international trade. The PLA made a profit every year, recording a net surplus in 1913–14 of £283,000 (almost £19.5 million today). The volume of cargo handled reached a record 20 million tons in 1913, although by then London's position as the world's premier port had been taken by Hamburg. The German port, free from duties and taxes, handled 25 million tons of cargo in 1912.

Economic prosperity was encouraging the forces of organised labour in the UK to flex their muscles. The PLA had adopted the labour system used by the London & India Docks Company. This consisted of four classes of labour: a body of permanent labourers, enjoying regular work and decent conditions and pay of 24 shillings a week; an 'A' list (abolished at the start of the First World War) of registered labourers, also enjoying regular work

and decent pay, but without disablement pension or sick pay; a 'B' list of preference labourers, known as 'prefs', earning 6d an hour and a minimum daily wage of 2 shillings, other than those engaged just for the afternoon; and the 'C' list, made up of casuals without any status. The PLA wanted other port employers to adopt the scheme as a way of reducing the need for casual labour but there was considerable resistance. The 1908 Act gave the PLA the responsibility for encouraging better labour conditions throughout the Port but the Authority could rely only on persuasion. With other employers sitting on the PLA Board, it was unsurprising that these attempts failed. Many dockers also preferred the freedom of casual work to the constraints of permanent contracts.

The whole country was disrupted by various labour disputes during 1911–12. The Port suffered from two major strikes during this period. The first began in July 1911 when the dockers' union, and other unions in the newly created National Transport Workers Federation, submitted claims to their employers. After negotiations, a settlement, known as the Devonport Agreement, was hammered out. This was rejected by the men who demanded better terms, particularly regarding union recognition. Although Devonport resisted pressure from the government to do a deal, the Board of Trade stepped in as a conciliator and the men returned to work on 14 August after a number of changes had been made to the original agreement. For the dockers, working every day at serious risk of injury, and conscious of their critical role in keeping the trade of the nation flowing, these changes

included the valuable provision of an ambulance service and a promise, in the days before a universal health service, that those suffering illness or injury would receive care in the local hospitals.

This dispute created a great deal of mistrust on both sides and relationships remained tense. The strike in 1912 began in May with an inter-union dispute, when a lighterman from the Lightermen's Union refused to work with another from the Foreman Lightermen's Union. As the strike spread throughout the Port, the PLA, with other port employers, refused to become involved, on the grounds that neither the Authority nor any other employer had broken the 1911 agreement. The PLA believed the fault lay with the lightermen. Under the terms of the agreement, they should have referred the dispute to their own unions and remained at work. The PLA saw the hand of the National Transport Workers Federation, the predecessor of the Transport and General Workers Union, in all of this. It blamed both strikes on the Federation's demand for all port employees to belong to unions affiliated to it, which the employers resisted.

With the port under pressure, the government intervened again, but once more Devonport resolutely resisted this interference. A national strike called by the Federation won little support, non-union men were drafted into London and the tone of the dispute became much more bitter. Devonport, furious at the men's repudiation of the 1911 agreement, declared in a fit of anger that he would starve them back to work. Ben Tillett, general secretary of the dockers' union, leading the men in prayer at a mass meeting on Tower Hill, declared, 'O God, strike Lord Devonport dead.' From the crowd came the response, 'He shall die! He shall die!'

Devonport later wrote that he believed that the facts were 'the best refutation of the fiction that I was a malignant capitalistic ogre, seeking to devour the poor workers'. His record as MP for Devonport showed that he was not unsympathetic to the working man for he had taken it on himself to ensure that the views of the naval dockyard employees were represented in Parliament. In this

instance, he remained unbending. The strikers began drifting back to work and by the end of August the dispute was over. Two of the leaders of the 1911 and 1912 strikes were both members of the PLA Board – Harry Gosling of the Lightermen's Union and James Anderson of the Stevedores' Society. By 1913, in response to the union and thanks to the prosperity of the Port, the PLA had increased its own permanent dock labour force to 3,000 men.

The Port was crucial to the country's war effort throughout the conflict. In 1914 the PLA's engineers took just 40 days to throw a temporary pontoon bridge, supported on 70 lighters, across the Thames at Gravesend. A similar structure had been placed across the river during an earlier invasion scare in 1588. In 1914 the bridge was

A police escorted convoy leaves the Royal Albert Dock during the long and bitter dock strike of 1912.

The Coat of Arms of the PLA.

FLOREAT · IMPERII · PORTUS

IMPERIAL PRESENCE

In 1909, the PLA was confronted with many challenges. Amongst these was the need to create a strong public image and to unify its disparate staff. It rose to the challenge in two ways. The first was the creation of a coat of arms, approved by King Edward VII. At the centre of the arms was a shield containing the image of St Paul, the patron saint of London. Above the shield was a knight's helmet supporting an 'Ancient Ship', whose mainsail bore the City of London cross. On either side, two mythical 'Sea Lions' held the Royal Standards of Kings Edward II and Edward VII. Charged with historic sentiment and symbolism, the arms bore the dedication 'Floreat Imperii Portus' – which translated as 'May the Imperial Port Flourish'. The Royal Warrant itself recognised London as the 'Principal Port of Our Empire'.

The imperial theme also characterised the second, more public, image of the PLA – the Head Offices at Trinity Square.

Although powers were given to clear the site – which included the PLA's own old East India Company Crutched Friars Warehouse, as well as many fine eighteenth-century houses – in 1911–1912, the First World War delayed construction. Sir Edwin Cooper's magnificent contribution to London's imperial architecture – built by John Mowlem & Company – was formally opened on 17 October 1922.

At the opening, Lord Devonport drew a parallel with the building of the West India Dock and stressed the area's history. Lloyd George reflected on the creation of the PLA and said that the new building was destined to 'be the centre of activity of a port which is the pride of our race in all our lands'. The building's façade was adorned with allegorical figures of 'Produce', 'Commerce', 'Exportation', 'Navigation' and – fittingly pointing his trident towards the river – 'Father Thames'.

The war memorial unveiled at Trinity Square in January 1926 to commemorate the lives of the 402 members of the PLA staff lost in the First World War.

More than 3,600 PLA staff joined the forces in the First World War and 402 either died or were killed in action. Two won the Victoria Cross – A G Drake, a labouring boy from the Town Warehouses, as a corporal in the Rifle Brigade in 1915; and E K Myles, a Fourth Class Clerk from the Royal Albert Dock, when a 2nd Lieutenant in the Welsh Regiment in 1916.

While many clerks who joined up gained commissions, most dockers who went in as privates came out as privates; the exception was permanent labourer W E Benham, killed in action in November 1918 as a 2nd Lieutenant.

Nine staff died in air raids on London and six died in the Silvertown explosion on 19 January 1917.

As well as two VCs, the awards received by PLA staff included one Distinguished Service Order, one Distinguished Service Cross, 25 Military Crosses, one Distinguished Flying Cross, 11 Distinguished Conduct Medals, two Distinguished Service Medals, and 47 Military Medals.

designed to protect important naval installations upstream, including a victualling depot, as well as the commercial docks. Taking into account the tides and currents of the river, the bridge was partly opened to shipping for three hours on each tide. The deck was strong enough to carry the weight of troops, cavalry, lorries or heavy artillery.

Although the dockers were exempt from conscription because of their value to the war effort, many of them joined up. Some of them served in the first Transport Workers' Battalions, of the 16th York and Lancaster Regiment, the forerunners of the Port Operating Groups that formed part of the Royal Engineers in the Second World War. Initially these volunteers worked in UK ports but by 1918 many of the 5,000 dockers in uniform were employed in French ports.

In the early part of the war, trade through London had been busier than ever, following the closure of the Continental ports. By 1915 the PLA's own labour force had almost doubled. In that year German aircraft and Zeppelins bombed the docks for the first time. Two years later, in January 1917, the brick and wooden warehouses and timber quays of the Royal Victoria Dock were badly damaged by the explosion at Brunner-Mond's nearby explosive works at Silvertown, the worst incident along the river during the war. In the same year, as the blockade by German submarines took effect, shipping was redirected under naval escort to ports on the west coast, and the queuing and congestion common in the Port during the first half of the war vanished. By 1916 New York claimed to have outstripped London in terms of the total value of port trade and by 1918 London's trade had fallen to half pre-war levels.

Peace brought a massive but short-lived boom in trade. Net registered tonnage entering and leaving the Port rose from just 15 million tons in 1918 to 33 million in 1920, although this was still below the figure for 1914. As a result, the PLA again increased its permanent labour force, which reached 4,500 by the end of 1920. Brief prosperity brought better wages and a shorter working week for London's dockworkers. The fear of droves of demobbed

During the war the PLA organised cruises down the river for convalescing troops from 1916 onwards.
This was how the PLA's river cruises, later revived for the general public in 1931, first began.

servicemen making their way to the docks in search of work encouraged renewed efforts to find a solution to the intractable problem of casual labour. In 1920 the Shaw Inquiry, the first of many similar inquiries, recommended the universal adoption of a system of registered dock labour, already practised in other UK ports, and accepted the principle of paying dockers an allowance even when they were without work. Here were the outlines of the future National Dock Labour Scheme, still a generation away. In 1921, with 61,000 newly registered dock workers in the Port, when the weekly average actually working was just 34,000, the real problem was too many men chasing too little work.

A more optimistic sign was the resumption of the capital programme delayed by the war. Grand arrangements were made for the opening of the King George V Dock, the first new dock since Tilbury in 1886. Eight thousand guests were invited to see the King perform the ceremony on 8 July 1921. As the King and Queen sailed down the river to the new dock, the banks of the Thames were lined with groups of school children, riverside premises were gaily decorated and vessels along the river and in every dock were fully dressed with flags and bunting. Epitomising the latest in dock design, with its modern warehouses, electric cranes, wide roads and extensive railway network, it was a clear sign of the PLA's confidence in the future of the Port. It was a confidence admired by others across the globe. In the same year the model of the PLA's 1908 constitution formed the template for the new Port Authority of New York.

The railway ran from the Tilbury Docks straight into the vast warehouses at Commercial Road, seen here around 1910, linking the docks to the City of London.

The royal opening of the King George V Dock in 1921 signalled the confidence of the PLA after the First World War.

Lord Ritchie of Dundee, the second Chairman of the PLA (1925-1941), on board the PLA launch, *Nore*, with the Sultan of Muscat in the 1930s. As one of the leading port authorities in the world, the PLA was regularly visited by heads of state and other foreign dignitaries.

1921–1939

Between the wars the PLA, guided by the first of its great General Managers, David Owen, continued to invest in the Port. During the 1920s works delayed or postponed by the First World War were completed. This programme was sustained during the difficult 1930s, partly through government assistance. The nationwide registration of dockers was introduced and the PLA did its utmost to keep its permanent labour force employed during the depression. Despite the downturn in trade, London remained an important international port, and began promoting itself seriously around the world for the first time. By the late 1930s, the Port accounted for a greater share of UK trade than ever before.

Lord Devonport handed over the chairmanship of the PLA to Lord Ritchie of Dundee in 1925. Ritchie, the head of a firm of East India merchants, had been Devonport's long-serving Vice-Chairman. They had not seen eye to eye. According to Devonport, Ritchie was inclined to caution, forever trying to rein in Devonport's expansive plans. Under Devonport, Ritchie had been given particular responsibility for the PLA's management of the river. While he had helped to persuade the Admiralty to invest in a new supply depot at Deptford in 1916–17, he had also rejected as too expensive major dredging proposals originally put forward in 1900. These had included plans for a second dredged channel along the route of the Princes Channel on the south of the Thames and would have improved deep water access to Tilbury and Canvey Island.

Ritchie's financial prudence proved justified as economic conditions deteriorated during the late 1920s and early 1930s. On the other hand, he had a keen eye for developments that would enhance port trade. He appreciated the commercial value of Tilbury and Canvey

Island. Devonport had not, preventing his Chief Engineers, Palmer and Kirkpatrick, from concentrating their planned investment downriver. Ritchie recognised the growing importance of the petroleum trade, which would result in the development of two oil terminals on the north bank of the river, close to Shell Haven and Hole Haven creeks. At his urging, the limits for the carriage of petroleum on the river were altered to accommodate Esso at Purfleet, securing what became the PLA's largest industrial customer. Another major new customer encouraged by Ritchie was

Sir David Owen, General Manager of the PLA from 1922 to 1938, was the first General Manager to make his mark on the Authority.

the Ford Motor Company, which constructed a huge concrete wharf alongside the factory it built at Dagenham between 1929 and 1931.

Working alongside Ritchie was David Owen, the Authority's General Manager. Owen, who was later knighted, came to the PLA in 1922 from Belfast, where he had been general manager of the Harbour Commission. Under his direction, most of Palmer's original proposals were taken up and major works were undertaken at almost all the Authority's docks, from new sheds at the Surrey Commercial Docks in the 1920s to the deepening of the Royal Victoria and Royal Albert Docks in the 1930s.

Although the depression compelled the Authority to curtail its original plans, some works were carried out with special government funding.

The Port had suffered in particular from the impact of the General Strike and then from the collapse of colonial economies during the depression. Indian trade, for instance, declined by half between 1925 and 1931. During this period of economic hardship, the PLA, as navigation authority, recognised its responsibility to encourage trade within the Port and cut rates, charges and dues twice. Yet the Authority was still able to introduce modern plant and equipment on the quayside and in the sheds and

A typical scene from the docks, tallying casks to marks and numbers, in 1931, with the tally clerk, shown in his cap on the right hand side, surrounded by dockers in their 'uniform' of jackets, waistcoats, ties and caps. (Linney Collection, Museum in Docklands)

warehouses. Along the river major dredging did take place in the 1920s and the Authority took a leading role in tackling worsening pollution caused by discharges from sewage works and riverside power stations. On a busy river populated by ships lacking sophisticated navigation equipment, the PLA also made a series of safety improvements, such as new byelaws to improve the safety and control of the carriage of petroleum.

A reduction in Port rates was possible partly because the PLA cut the dockers' wages. The PLA was the Port's largest single employer, with half of its 12,000-strong workforce made up of dockers, although this was less than ten per cent of all registered dock labour in the Port. Wage increases made at the end of the war were steadily eroded by a series of cuts during the 1920s and

1930s, a policy followed by many other employers up and down the country. Strikes over hours took place in 1923 and again in 1924. A further enquiry was set up to look into the casual labour system but its chairman, Sir Donald Maclean, another eminent judge, reached much the same conclusions as Shaw had done.

In 1926 almost all the PLA's dockers took part in the General Strike. The Port was designated as a special area with its own commissioner, Colonel Brabazon-Moore, the parliamentary secretary at the Ministry of Transport. The Authority expected heavy picketing in such a strongly

Armed troops and police preparing to lead a major food convoy out of the Royal Albert Dock during disruption caused by the the 1926 General Strike.

A dock constable searching a loaded timber cart leaving the Surrey Commercial Docks, around 1930.
Thefts rose during the terrible years of the depression when so many were out of work. (Linney Collection, Museum in Docklands)

working-class area so police protection was provided, the Admiralty sent in two destroyers, and military escorts guarded food convoys, loaded in the Royal Albert Dock by more than 1,200 volunteers. When the borough council of West Ham, sympathetic to the strikers, threatened to cut off electricity in the docks, the Admiralty, in a remarkable operation, towed two submerged Royal Navy submarines to the entrance of the King George V Dock. Engineers connected the submarines' generators to the PLA's cold stores, preventing their valuable food stocks, including 750,000 carcasses of frozen meat, from defrosting.

Labour was in a much weaker position during the depressed 1930s. By 1931, the number of registered dockers in the Port had fallen to 37,000, daily unemployment was around 30 per cent and pay rates had dropped by a quarter since 1921. The Authority was sympathetic towards the plight of those who had been left out of work but little could be done for the hungry army of casual labourers. One dock manager recalled how several hundred men would fight over a dozen jobs. This was a time when poverty in the local neighbourhoods was so

The PLA operated an extensive rail network which was particularly important for the carriage of freight. This photo depicts a busy scene in the West India Dock during the 1930s.

Salvage is an important part of the PLA's responsibilities. Here a PLA salvage diver attends the scene of a wreck in 1934.

severe that undernourished young children often stole from carts carrying foodstuffs out of the docks. As for the 'perms', sometimes there was so little dock work that they were sent to clean warehouse windows.

To avoid dismissing men, the Authority adopted the 'stand-off' system. Each dock was allocated a quota of men to be stood off day by day, every 'perm' standing off in strict rotation so what little work there was could be shared out fairly. New legislation gave the Authority additional responsibilities for staff pensions and this stimulated debate over the provision of pensions for dockworkers. The idea was first raised in 1934 but was eventually shelved in 1937. Blue-collar pension schemes were rare but a more enlightened approach may have helped to lessen the ultimate costs of the National Dock Labour Scheme half a century later. Despite this omission, the Authority did increase pay and piecework rates, in 1935 and 1937. The union appreciated the 'stand-off' scheme so, with better times, the two sides tried in the late 1930s to draw up a scheme to decasualise labour in the

A set of cartons being discharged in the Royal Victoria Dock in 1935 as trade began to recover after the Depression. The Royal Docks were regarded as the jewel in the PLA's crown as far as handling cargo was concerned.

Port; once again this foundered on the reluctance of other London riverside employers to take part.

Despite continued progress in the Port of London, there were critics who advocated not just single authorities for each port but one national port authority to overcome what they saw as the failure of so many of the diversely governed UK ports to meet the needs of modern shipping. It was feared any revival in trade would leave port authorities at a disadvantage, since the cost of developing deep docks was prohibitive and suitable sites were

hard to find. Ship-owners were reluctant to invest in larger vessels which would only take longer to discharge in port and thus incur higher charges. Ultimately a later revolution in handling cargo would sweep away archaic labour-intensive methods. There were already signs of this before the Second World War as the railway companies developed movable containers that could be mounted on rail wagons. Although they were unsuitable for orthodox cargo-handling operations in the docks, they proved successful on specially built railway ferries. In 1927 a quay in Tilbury's enlarged

tidal basin was allocated to the London, Midland & Scottish Railway Company for a nightly container service to Dunkirk. Other services operated from Harwich and Dover.

The Port of London was still the country's most important port. It was also regarded as one of the most efficient port authorities in the country, along with Liverpool and the Clyde ports. London was handling almost twice as much shipping tonnage as the next largest port (Liverpool), while the value of exports and imports in the Port was worth more than those of Liverpool, Hull, Southampton and Manchester put together. The investment made by the PLA had helped to steer the Port safely through the depression. Although the country's export trade slumped to half the level of 1914, imports increased

During the depressed 1930s, when many dockers had no work, and their families lived in poverty, those fortunate to retain employment within the PLA often did their best to provide help. The PLA police were particularly active and this scene shows a group of children departing from the Royal Victoria Dock in 1932 on an outing to Burnham Beaches organised by the police benevolent fund.

as world prices fell. This helped the net registered tonnage of vessels entering and leaving the Port to rise steadily. They exceeded pre-war levels in 1927, reaching 57.5 million net registered tons, and rose to 63 million tons in 1938. London's share of UK trade rose to 38 per cent, an achievement which has never yet been surpassed. Much of this stemmed from the business produced by the growing petroleum and car industries, which Lord Ritchie had been instrumental in attracting to the river. The Port of London's success was also achieved at a time when the UK's share of world trade was in decline.

Although New York had taken the title of the world's busiest port, London retained a leading international reputation. This was consolidated during the late 1920s and throughout the 1930s thanks to the work of the PLA's publicity department. This was formed in 1929 when A E Wildey was appointed the PLA's public relations officer. Representatives were appointed overseas and promotional visits were made to ports in Australasia, Canada and South America. A magazine, *The PLA Monthly*, was founded, and, among several promotional films about the Port commissioned by the Authority, the most impressive was *City of Ships*, made in 1938.

Sir David Owen, who had steered the PLA successfully through difficult times, retired in 1938. J Douglas Ritchie was appointed to succeed him as General Manager. A solicitor who had worked in local government, Ritchie joined the PLA in 1923, later becoming the Authority's Solicitor and Secretary. It would be his task to lead the Authority through the dangerous waters of the Second World War.

The opening of the Tilbury passenger landing stage by the Prime Minister, Ramsay MacDonald, seen here mooring the first ship, on 16 May 1930 was a major investment for the Port. The presence of leading politicians and members of the royal family on these occasions was an indication of the high status of the PLA.

These paintings (this page and opposite) by William Hain vividly depict the night-time bombing raids on the docks during the Blitz. (Courtesy of the Museum of London)

1939–1945

The Second World War once again found the PLA at the heart of the nation's war effort. The Port not only remained an important distribution centre for crucial supplies of food and other goods, it was a focal point for two of the key events of the war. The PLA's workforce made an enormous, and in some cases heroic, contribution but the Port itself paid a high price. By the end of the war, many of the docks had been devastated by bombing.

Douglas Ritchie, who would be knighted for his wartime services to the Port, proved an outstanding leader. In particular he displayed a sensitivity that was much appreciated at a time when the Port was battered and bruised. Under him, the PLA prepared as best it could for the outbreak of war. Alternative premises for female office staff were found safely upstream in Thames Ditton, a wartime administration scheme was drawn up, and the River Emergency Service was formed. On the day war was declared, every port in the country came under the control of Port Emergency Committees (PEC). In London this was effectively the PLA. The river and the docks were dressed for war. Naval guardships were placed at the seaward limit of the river, where the great Maunsell Sea Forts were later erected on stilts. Gun batteries were sited on both banks of the lower river and guns

installed at lock gates and other key points. Pill boxes and shelters appeared around the docks. Barrage balloons, many of them secured to lighters, floated above the docks and industrial areas of the river's middle reaches. The PLA survey vessel, *St Katharine*, with a six-pounder gun installed, was the first vessel on the river to open fire on the enemy after war had been declared, when German planes attempted to mine the river.

On Saturday 7 September 1940 the first bombs fell on the Port of London. Eighteen-year-old PLA employee Cyril Webb was due on duty that evening at Surrey Commercial Docks. As he left home on his bicycle, the glorious summer weather was marred only by what seemed an unusual black cloud on the horizon. The cloud turned out to be a swarm of 375 German bombers. The docks were already ablaze by the time Webb reached them. Fuelled by vast stocks of timber, the fires burned for five days. In the Quebec Dock the blaze was the single most fierce ever recorded in the UK.

In burning warehouses around the docks, rubber, paint, flour and pepper burst into flames, rum barrels exploded and parts of the river, covered in liquid sugar, caught alight. The heat was so intense that the paint blistered on craft creeping along the river. The fire officer in charge reported that 'The whole bloody world's on fire'. By the time the last of the bombers headed back over the Channel in the early hours of the morning, 430 civilians had died and much of the Port's infrastructure had been shattered.

For 76 nights the tidal river was under continuous attack. The Blitz reduced trade in the Port to a quarter of its pre-war level. The PLA's male staff found themselves

The colossal blaze at Surrey Commercial Docks on 7-8 September 1940, with thousands of tons of timber on fire.
Remarkably, there was only one fatality in the docks.

under the command of the Royal Navy's Flag Officer for London and his team. Military Police occupied the docks. PLA tugs formed part of the River Fire Patrol and the Admiralty asked the Authority to extend its wreck salvage operations into the estuary. Staff started the Port of London House Group of the Local Defence Volunteers, later renamed the Home Guard. Work began in the docks on the conversion of merchantmen into armed naval auxiliaries. Routine operations were abandoned as rail, road and inland water transport shipped vast quantities of food and raw materials to safer storage centres outside the Port. The permanent closure of some of the old upper docks was even considered. The role of the Port changed as it became the principal junction between the west-coast ports, where convoys brought in their supplies, and the metropolis and its vast hinterland. PLA warehousing staff helped to organise depots for evacuated foodstuffs in safer areas, such as Watford. At the same time, as the

Douglas Ritchie, PLA General Manager from 1938 to 1946, on the left, touring the docks in September 1940 with the Prime Minister, Winston Churchill, Mrs Churchill and the Flag Officer, London, Rear-Admiral Boyle. Here they are with a group of auxiliary firemen.

Battle of the Atlantic was under way, goods were also despatched by train from Liverpool and Glasgow to the PLA's London warehouses. As part of the policy of dispersing valuable goods, the PLA obtained a number of petroleum barges, moored in the river with their valuable cargo.

The docks became particularly dangerous places in which to work. There were many acts of remarkable bravery. Policemen moved ammunition from burning warehouses, dockers extinguished incendiary bombs in warehouses full of inflammable goods, dock railway staff isolated blazing wagons containing explosives and ammunition, dockmasters and their staff deployed their tugs to save ships and other craft in danger. Throughout this terrible time the men and women of the PLA kept the Port going in the most difficult conditions. They fought

In peacetime few women were employed by the PLA outside the dock offices but they came into their own during the Second World War. This image shows three volunteers of the River Emergency Service, with bandages, blackout torches and splints, during Civil Defence training.

fires, rescued cargo, administered first aid, saved lives and served as wardens, snatching sleep whenever they could. Many ordinary people did some extraordinary things.

Lives were often lost. The list of fatal civilian casualties recorded in the PLA's monthly magazine grew longer with each issue. In September 1940 one police sergeant, C E Showell, was fatally injured and his constable, R C Whinney, killed, when an unexploded bomb went off as they tried to unlock a shed to let in the fire service to tackle the blaze. One of the worst incidents occurred in November 1940, when a parachute mine landed in Tilbury Dock and destroyed two PLA tugs, the *Deanbrook* and the *Lea*. Eleven men were killed – from the *Deanbrook*, these were the master, J Gilbert; P Stickland, engineer; W Stoner,

A detachment of the PLA Local Defence Volunteers, later the Home Guard, training at the Royal Docks in 1940.

The warehouses of the Eastern Basin, St Katharine Docks, well ablaze during the Blitz of September 1940.
By the end of the war the docks had been devastated by enemy action, leaving the PLA with a huge repair bill.

In the aftermath of the Blitz, precious sugar is salvaged from the remains of No 7 Warehouse, North Quay, West India Docks.

driver; C Whale, stoker; and W W Gallichan, deckhand; those who died on board the *Lea* were A E Jeffery, master; A Hayman, driver; J Hyde, stoker; H Atkinson, stoker; W G Horn, deckhand; and A Rathbone, deckhand.

There was little respite from the bombing until the end of May 1941. By then, the magnificent rotunda gracing the PLA's head office in Trinity Square had also fallen victim to enemy action.

Once again the dockers were seen as indispensable to the war effort. In the West India Dock, where the PLA employed its own gangs to discharge ships, dockers worked from 8 am to 7 pm six days a week and until 5 pm on Sundays. Many of them were middle-aged and elderly, sustained only by wartime rations. It was these men who helped to recover 61,000 tons of sugar for human consumption from what was left of the North Quay warehouses in 1940. Elsewhere in the docks, once the worst of the bombing was over in 1941, salvage work began on the burned-out warehouses. Coasters ferried tons of scrap metal to smelting works and rubble was used for the foundations of wartime airfields.

Recognising the value of the dockers, the government, under the Essential Work (General Provisions) Order (EWO), 1941, introduced compulsory registration. As a quid pro quo, supported by Ernest Bevin, now Minister of Labour, every registered dock worker in every port was given regular employment with a guaranteed wage, and the National Dock Labour Corporation was established to administer the scheme.

The bomb-damaged façade of Trinity Square, protected by barbed wire across the entrance steps, with windows and doors blown out, and some windows bricked up. The inner rotunda was destroyed.

The EWO also gave the government the power to direct any docker to any port in the country. Some PLA dockers, with other dockers and stevedores, had already left London for the Clyde where Robert Letch, the assistant to the PLA's General Manager, had been asked to organise the Clyde Emergency Anchorages. The first 75 PLA dockers in a group that would eventually total 500 went up with their families in September 1940. At the Emergency Anchorages Port off Gourock, these men helped to discharge cargoes from ships into coasters for transhipment to other ports. The PLA also sent up cranes, trucks and 300 Thames dumb barges. Letch, successively Regional Port Director for the Clyde Ports, Scotland and the North West of England, was knighted for his contribution.

Later in the conflict, a Norwegian war correspondent attached to the British merchant navy summed up the contribution of London's dockers. He wrote how:

A dramatic painting by William Ware of large wharves ablaze along the river in 1940. (By courtesy of the artist's family. On loan to the Museum in Docklands)

'Before the war these dock workers, according to their own custom, would stop work as soon as there was a drop of rain. Now when I was down in the Port of London I saw 'fly-bombs' coming over and did they stop work? Why, the dockers didn't even look at them. They just went on so that the ship could sail the same night. That's the spirit of the dock workers of London today.'

That spirit was reflected in the handfuls of the newly instituted George Medal for civilian gallantry awarded to PLA employees. One of them was Henry Hook, a PLA perm, who won his medal in 1944. He crawled under a burning railway truck full of petrol cans, uncoupled it and helped to move it away to prevent the fire spreading. Not content with this, he climbed onto another truck full of explosives to remove a tarpaulin covered in blazing debris.

Alongside the dockers, other PLA staff played a vital role in keeping the Port open. The salvage depart-ment cleared wrecks, rescued bombed ships, extinguished on-board fires and saved valuable cargo from damaged vessels. The PLA's *Yantlet* was complemented by the *King Lear*, on loan from a towage company, and by vessels from the Dover Harbour Board and the Admiralty. The Harbour Service turned the River Emergency Service into an efficient organisation, running ambulance vessels and tenders. Harbour Service personnel helped with minesweeping, set up wartime defences, marked wrecks or damaged wharves and piers with green flags, super-vised the River Tug Fire Patrol and supplied fresh water for ships and fuel for small craft. When the bombing of the capital was at its height, and many bus and underground routes were impassable, the PEC organised an emergency commuter service for the London Passenger Transport Board, using up-river pleasure steamers, supplemented by diesel and steam tugs.

The crucial role of the dockers to the war effort brought some improvement in their working conditions, including the introduction of mobile canteens. Here the staff of the PLA's Mobile Canteen No 32 dispense tea to dockers queueing up during one of their breaks.

THE DUNKIRK EVACUATION AND THE D-DAY LANDINGS

The Port was at the heart of two major wartime operations, the evacuation of Dunkirk and the D-Day landings.

For the rescue of British servicemen trapped at Dunkirk in 1940, Harbour Service staff brought together craft from all parts of the river. These ranged from spritsail barges, big ship tugs and private launches, to a sludge hopper, a Thames fire-float (the *Massey Shaw*) and countless lifeboats. *The PLA Monthly* described how 'deep-sea ships, colliers and general coasters, craft of all shapes and sizes, craft which had never before been out of the river, craft in which the carrying of passengers had never before been contemplated, all got under way'.

Station Officer Brian Court gets a welcome home kiss from his young daughter Joy as he arrives back from Dunkirk on 5 June 1940 with the *Massey Shaw*, one of the many valiant small ships to take part in the evacuation.
(Courtesy of AP Images)

On the Thames preparations for the D-Day invasion began at Tilbury Dock in 1942, where welding work started on what became PLUTO (Pipeline Under The Ocean). Tilbury also sent out the huge floating bobbins (known as 'conundrums', reflecting the secrecy of the project) that helped to lay the pipeline. In the docks and along the river countless patrol vessels, minesweepers, barges and landing craft were built and repaired, including at the purpose-built Denton slipways, near Gravesend, still in operation in 2009. The East India Import Dock and the South Dock of the Surrey Docks were pumped dry and used to build some of the 'Phoenix' concrete caissons for the Mulberry harbours. The East India Import Dock never reopened.

Forty-six of the 147 units ordered were assembled on the Thames. The closer the big day came, the more intense the activity along the river. The Americans took over a large part of the Royal Albert Dock. Field Marshal Montgomery addressed 16,000 London dockers in the spring of 1944, stressing their

The LCC Thames fire float, *Massey Shaw*, which made three journeys across the Channel and rescued 600 men from Dunkirk, returned home on 5 June 1940 to a rapturous reception from well-wishers.
(Courtesy of AP Images)

Tanks in the London Docks preparing for embarkation
for the D-Day landings in 1944.

crucial role in the next stage of the war. Dockers agreed to load military supplies around the clock and marshalling began in late May 1944. *The PLA Monthly* recorded how 'from the docks and wharves upstream a steady flow of deep-sea ships, coasters, tugs, barges, oilers and landing craft was joined in the estuary anchorages by flotillas of escort vessels'. On 6 June 1944, 209 ships, 194 of them loaded in London's docks, sailed down the Thames, accompanied by a thousand barges. Once the invasion got under way, London dockers in uniform worked on the completed harbours at Arromanches, off the Normandy coast.

(Opposite) British troops embarking for the D-Day invasion in June 1944 'somewhere in the docks'.

(Below) The last complete Phoenix Unit or Mulberry Harbour to leave the Port through the King George V Dock Entrance under tow in 1944 and heading for the D-Day beaches.

During the war more than 1,400 PLA staff served in the forces. Alfred Waker, 42 years a docker in London Docks, suffered the deaths on active service of three of his five sons, two of whom had been employed by the PLA. Many younger dockers, with the formation of the dozen PLA Dock Groups, became members of the Royal Engineers. They served at every point of action where shipping and port activity was involved, from North Africa to Sicily, from France to Burma. During the invasion of Sicily, one gang was still helping to discharge a vessel when she had to set sail while they were still aboard; it was a year before they returned. The contribution of all these men and women, including the 64 killed in action with the forces and the 61 who perished at work or in their homes, was commemorated in the memorial window unveiled by Lord Alanbrooke in the main entrance of Trinity Square in 1952.

At the end of the war the Port had been devastated. Thousands of incendiary bombs and over 900 high-explosive bombs and missiles had caused damage valued at £13.5 million based on pre-war prices (nearly £600 million at today's prices). Half of all storage and one-third of all warehousing in the docks had been lost. In Surrey Commercial Docks, 176 sheds had been completely destroyed and 57 others had to be demolished. Tarpaulins and prefabricated huts were used as makeshift cover for goods. Tilbury escaped without much damage, having been identified by the Germans for use after invasion, although incendiary bombs destroyed the famous Tilbury Hotel in 1944. The concrete structures erected in the Royal Docks during their rebuilding in the late 1930s also proved resilient, and most of them survived the bombs. Despite the best efforts of the PEC, dredging had been neglected and wrecks littered the estuary. With much of the Port's newer equipment despatched to other ports and destinations around the UK, at the end of the war the Port was handicapped by old and overworked machinery in a poor state of repair. Simply bringing the Port back into full operation would be a time-consuming and expensive task.

No.1 Berth, Tilbury, was constructed for the vessels of the P&O and Orient Lines in 1957.

1945–1967

It took the PLA a decade to complete the rebuilding of the Port after the destruction caused by the war. The Authority also had to take into account the gradual changes taking place in the shipping industry, as vessels increased in size and cargo-handling methods altered. Roll-on, roll-off (ro-ro) short sea ferries, palletised cargo and fork-lift trucks, packaged timber, unit loads and containers – these innovations were like a slow-burning fuse, adopted only gradually at first, but with an ultimately explosive impact upon every major port in the world. Adapting to these changes was not easy and the Authority faced opposition not just from the dockers but also from some staff. Industrial relations were tense, which the introduction of the National Dock Labour Scheme in 1947 did little to help. Just as the labour-saving method of containerisation was being widely adopted, the dockers finally achieved their aim of full decasualisation and a guaranteed minimum wage in 1967.

In January 1946 Thomas Wiles, the PLA's wartime Chairman, was succeeded by the supreme administrator of his age, Sir John Anderson, subsequently Viscount Waverley. A distinguished civil servant and

Sir John Anderson, later Viscount Waverley, was Chairman of the PLA from 1946 to 1958. He is seen here inspecting PLA police and recruits, with Chief Police Officer Simmons, at the training school in the Royal Docks in 1946.

The PLA Board in session at head office about 1945, with Thomas Wiles, PLA Chairman from 1941 until 1946, presiding.
The first PLA Board Meeting would have looked much the same.

wartime Home Secretary and Chancellor of the Exchequer, Waverley was so august that he was known as 'Jehovah' to his staff. When he was informed on the occasion of one of the frequent royal visits to the Port that umbrellas would be available in case of rain, he pronounced that it would not rain; nor did it, although it rained on each day either side of the visit.

Sir Douglas Ritchie, the General Manager, was replaced by Theo Williams, the Port's Dock and Traffic Manager, but Williams retired in 1948. To supervise the reconstruction of the Port, Waverley chose Leslie Ford, Chief Docks Manager in South Wales for the newly nationalised British Railways. Clever, thoughtful and autocratic, Ford, like his Chairman, excelled at administration, and together they oversaw the revival of the Port after the war.

Waverley died in 1958 and his place was taken in 1960 by Viscount Simon. A member of the PLA Board since 1950, who inherited his title from his father, the eminent politician, in 1954, he was an experienced shipping executive. He had served with MacKinnon MacKenzie before joining P&O and spent his war years with the Ministry of War Transport. After the war he rose to become Managing Director and Deputy Chairman of P&O. Like Lord Ritchie, Simon recognised the value to the Port of fuel cargoes and was supportive of the move to bring liquid petroleum gas into the Thames for the first time in 1959.

When Leslie Ford, the last holder of the post to receive the knighthood obligatory for General Managers since the days of David Owen, stepped down in 1964, he was succeeded by Dudley Perkins. Perkins, the PLA's Solicitor, was well known as the radio lawyer from his radio programme, *Can I Help You?*, during his time with the BBC. Despite his legal background, and some criticism of his management skills, Perkins was the man who recognised the magnitude of the impending changes in cargo handling and saved the Port from obsolescence.

Between 1947 and 1961 the PLA invested more than £108 million on long-overdue repairs and desperately needed rebuilding. This was a colossal sum of money, worth around £1,740 million today. It underlined the scale

Sir Leslie Ford, PLA General Manager from 1948 to 1964, played a key part in the reconstruction and revitalisation of the docks after the war.

A Morris car being loaded at the Royal Albert Dock in February 1949, part of a record consignment of vehicles bound for Singapore.
Exports brought in much needed foreign currency to a nation virtually bankrupted by the war.

of the task that had faced the PLA in 1945. With hindsight, some of this investment, failing to take into account the speed with which change was occurring in the port industry, was probably ill-judged. Rail facilities were modernised as the switch to road haulage was accelerating. An expensive new passenger terminal, opened at Tilbury in 1957, never fulfilled expectations as the age of air travel dawned.

On the other hand, Ford and a number of his senior managers did make the conscious decision to adapt the docks wherever possible to the changes in cargo handling. This was not always easy. Among some dock managers, there was a tendency to inertia. It did not help that promotion within the PLA was traditionally based as much on seniority as on merit. One younger manager, rising through the ranks in the 1950s, criticised some of his seniors for the way they 'clung so tenaciously to their small technical knowledge'. Their conservatism was an obstacle

to change. The modernisation of one major dock was apparently delayed for several years until the retirement of the incumbent dock superintendent, who was known to have little appetite for it. This frustrated the new generation of managers, men who during their wartime service had seen the impact made by the fork-lift trucks and mobile cranes used by their American allies.

Those in charge of the Authority knew just how important mechanisation was for the Port and in 1947 had formed a special committee to investigate this. As *The PLA Monthly* later put it, 'only a clean break with many long-cherished traditions would permit full use of the machine'. With an immediate post-war shortage of labour and a demand for even quicker turnaround times as the nation

Repairs underway to the quay near 'M' Shed
at South West India Dock in 1947.

The discharge of North American timber from the vessel *Tosca* in the busy and crowded Royal Docks in 1947. The PLA worked hard to sort out the problem of congestion.

went on an export drive, the Authority placed orders for more modern equipment, although deliveries were often delayed because of Britain's parlous post-war economic state. To make the most of these new machines, modern sheds were erected, broad and high, to stack the pallets handled by cranes and fork-lifts, with immediate benefits in productivity.

The PLA made other improvements, including dredging the main river channels to alleviate port congestion, especially in the Surrey Commercial Docks. In 1949 two new deep-water berths for larger vessels were created at the South Quay in the West India Import Dock. In the same year the principle of bulk handling, long established for grain, was extended to sugar. One small dock, the East India Import Dock, badly damaged following its use to build Mulberry Harbours, had been closed in 1946. The site was sold for the construction of the Brunswick Wharf power station, which became an important customer of the PLA, with revenues raised from the cargoes of coal brought in to fuel the station. The Authority was limited by cash constraints in how much it could achieve and many projects, including two new concrete-framed

Viscount Simon, PLA Chairman from 1958 to 1971, son of the Liberal politician, Sir John Simon, was an experienced shipping executive who worked hard to modernise the Port.

and discharged in the PLA's docks. The Port was so busy that congestion was a major problem for the timber and other seasonal trades, with ships queuing up to enter the docks. One member of staff at Trinity Square, who had the daily task in the early 1960s of adding the names of ships in dock to a magnetised map of the Port in the Chairman's Conference Room, recalled once putting up 180 names. So many ships were passing through the entrance lock to the Royal Docks that the nearby Dock Office was in almost perpetual shade from the shadows cast by vessels on their way through. Yet, while London continued to be the UK's leading port, it never regained the position of the premier port worldwide. Rotterdam, which had surpassed it in tonnage terms by the mid-1950s, handled three times as much trade by the late 1960s, and by 1970 had become the world's leading port in terms of cargo tonnage, a position it held until it was overtaken by Singapore in 1992. Since then Far Eastern ports have dominated the league table, currently headed by Shanghai.

The trends driving change in the docks affected the river too, where the PLA was the navigation authority. Ever-larger vessels demanded deeper channels, dredged by the PLA. Larger ships made safety on the river even more important and the PLA was at the forefront in adopting the latest technology. One innovation was the world's first purpose-designed port navigation and information service, the Thames Navigation Service (TNS), launched in 1959 and based at Gravesend.

warehouses built between 1950 and 1954, were funded by war-damage compensation.

As the world economy improved, all these changes helped London to attract more trade than ever. In 1947 just 33 million tons of cargo had passed through the Port; in 1964 the Port achieved more than 61 million tons (62 million tonnes), a post-war record, accounting for almost a third of all UK trade. Excluding coal and oil, two-thirds of the Port's total exports and imports were loaded

Dudley Perkins, PLA General Manager from 1964 to 1970, was confronted with decasualisation and the container revolution during one of the Port's most difficult periods.

a much increased and more complex trade, with the ports of 50 years ago'.

After a review of the long term needs of the Port, a multi-million pound modernisation programme, phased over several years, went ahead. This concentrated on Tilbury, the Royal Docks and the West India and Millwall Docks. The first stage of the programme for Tilbury had been completed and plans for the second stage were well advanced when the Authority had a sudden change of mind.

The crucial decision was made by Ford's successor, Dudley Perkins. On a fact-finding mission to New York in February 1964, he saw at first hand the impact of containerisation at Port Elizabeth. The speed and efficiency of the operation was a revelation. He immediately sent a telegram to Trinity Square, putting the original plans for the modernisation of Tilbury on hold until his return. Perkins believed he could pre-empt the loss of London trade to near Continental ports, such as Rotterdam and Antwerp, by adapting the Port for handling containers. Perkins' views were not universally supported. Many dock managers failed to see the advantages of containerisation. Yet Albert Tooth, the PLA's legal advisor, supported by the PLA's professional engineers, had headed from 1954 until 1957 the International Standards Committee that had agreed the sizes and fixing devices for international container traffic. Perkins was also fortunate that those who did support his view were an influential group. With this backing, Perkins had persuaded the PLA

By the early 1960s, with post-war reconstruction complete, Simon and Ford could look to the future. They recognised the need to invest in new docks as cargo-handling methods changed. The 1962 Rochdale report into UK ports pointed out there had been no new deep-water berths in the UK, other than at Teesport, since the 1930s. The last new dock in London had been the King George V in 1921. The PLA's Vice-Chairman, Sir Andrew Crichton, complained in 1965 that 'We are endeavouring to handle the trade of the second half of the twentieth century,

The proliferation of cranes, lighters and shipping in the Royal Albert Docks in 1964 – the peak post-war year for the tonnage of cargo handled in the Port gives no indication of the imminent cargo-handling revolution.

Board to press ahead with provision for containerisation by mid-1965. This decision would add the UK's first major fully integrated container-ship terminal to Tilbury's existing facilities. New deep-water berths, designed to accommodate the bigger container ships, were expected to handle an annual throughput of between 500,000 and 1,000,000 tons of cargo, compared with 100,000 tons every year for a conventional cargo berth.

It was obvious from the outset that these changes would reduce the demand for dock labour. The PLA's first mechanised export berth at South Dock in the West India Docks in 1951 had slashed by two-thirds the number of men required. The dockers opposed many of these initiatives because of their impact on jobs. The PLA, through two executives, Stan Turner and Dick Butler, arranged for parties of dockers to visit Continental ports. In Rotterdam the dockers saw for themselves how much cargo was bypassing London through transhipment to smaller English ports. Although this persuaded them to sign up for the agreement to handle container vessels for US Lines at Tilbury, many other dockers were reluctant to believe that London would be seriously affected by this revolution.

The PLA, by far the Port's single largest employer, was not immune from the fraught labour relations which dogged port operations after 1945. This situation stemmed partly from the National Dock Labour Scheme, based on the wartime scheme and introduced in 1947. Many casual workers, despite the fact that they had often been short of work, resented the way the Scheme infringed their freedom of action. It also loosened the mutual bonds between docker and dock employer. Casual workers, allocated to a dock labour pool, were assigned to employers in proportion to the number of those employers' permanent dock labourers. Employers could not choose the labour they were given, nor the dockers the employer to whom they were sent. With little loyalty to any one employer, there was less compunction about going on strike. The Scheme was also criticised for its weak disciplinary procedures, which were under the joint control of unions and employers.

The Port was plagued by strikes after the war. There were 37 strikes between 1945 and 1955 and 93 between 1964 and 1966. Since there were almost 400 employers of dock labour in the Port in the early 1960s, the potential for disputes was enormous. Action by any one group of workers could cause chaos and such disputes could spread rapidly. The tally clerks' strike in 1960 lasted from September into October, caused the diversion of nearly 200 vessels to other ports, and lost the Port permanent business. Yet London was not the worst of the UK ports in the National Dock Labour Scheme for days lost at work – Liverpool's record was significantly worse.

Strikes had many causes although they were usually linked to wages and working arrangements. The willingness of shipping companies, whose vessels were either stranded in dock or queuing to get in, to concede the dockers' demands aggravated the difficulties faced by stevedoring and lighterage companies. Many dockers had little trust in their national and district union leaders, so most of the action was unofficial, placing it outside formal union control.

The large number of unofficial strikes and stoppages precipitated yet more formal enquiries into labour relations within the port industry. The consensus, embodied in the second Devlin report of 1966, was for the complete decasualisation of the dock labour force. This was not opposed by employers who believed a permanent workforce would be more receptive to change. Devlin's recommendations, supported by the Labour government, were implemented in 1967. As well as increasing the permanent labour forces of every Port employer, they also made it impossible for compulsory redundancies to take place. Such burdens boosted the prospects of ports like Felixstowe, which lay outside the National Dock Labour Scheme. Implementation also coincided with the devaluation of sterling, partly as a result of the damage to the country's balance of payments caused by the seamen's strike in 1966. Above all, it was already becoming obvious that modern cargo handling methods needed far fewer dockworkers.

Gordon's London Gin for export being loaded from a barge into a ship at the Royal Docks in 1959.

A view across to the enclosed dock at Tilbury in the 1990s. The privatisation of Tilbury in 1992 ended the direct links between the PLA and the enclosed docks that had existed since 1909.

1967–1992

During the next 25 years the PLA underwent a slow and painful transformation. As shipping companies adopted the new ways of handling cargo, work for the PLA's traditional enclosed docks dwindled. The first major dock closures took place in 1967, the last were announced in 1980. Tilbury was the sole survivor, bolstered by the growth of its modern container-handling operations. All this caused a sharp decline in the demand for registered dock labour in the Port. Reduced conventional cargo tonnages, the loss of transhipment trade to European ports, winding down the docks, paying off the workforce, investing in Tilbury and keeping river dues at moderate levels all impoverished the PLA. Nor was the PLA able to realise full development value for the land made available after the closure of the docks. Successive governments, while expecting the cash-strapped PLA to adopt a more commercial approach, refused to reform the National Dock Labour Scheme. The Authority continued to manage the river with success and in 1988 acquired responsibility for marine pilots. In 1989 the abolition of the Dock Labour Scheme paved the way for the privatisation of Tilbury Docks in 1992. Without the expense of operating the docks, the PLA could concentrate more fully on the river.

In response to declining trade, the first docks the PLA closed were the East India Export Dock and the London and St Katharine

The revolution that swept through the docks is summed up in this image - 'M' Shed, later renamed No.19 Shed, in South West India Dock, provided modern facilities for the Ben Line when it was opened in October 1967 but was demolished just 17 years later by the London Docklands Development Corporation.

Docks in 1967 and 1968 respectively. Surrey Commercial Docks followed in 1970, West India and Millwall Docks in 1980 and the Royal Docks in 1981. The once august PLA visibly shrank. Trinity Square, the Authority's imposing headquarters, was sold in 1971 less than 50 years after it had been opened. The Authority moved to the much smaller St Katharine House, an inconspicuous and undistinguished building in the old dock, which combined with another building to become known as the World Trade Centre. There were fewer Board members as ties with the original representative bodies were cut, with non-executives recruited on merit, and places were reserved for senior executives.

Tilbury quickly established a reputation for handling packaged timber. Several more specialist berths were added, increasing Tilbury's capacity in 1962 to more than a million tonnes a year. At their peak the Surrey Commercial Docks had a capacity of just 800,000 tons a

The building of the Bulk Grain Terminal at Tilbury, opened in 1969, was part of the programme of modernisation planned by the PLA to give the Port a future after the advent of the container revolution. Behind the terminal, seen here in 1979, are the great concrete aprons designed for container storage. (Courtesy of Handford)

year. Although industrial action affected Tilbury's development as a container port, more than half of all containers passing through the Port were landed at Tilbury by the mid-1970s. A decade later, Tilbury was described as a complete port in its own right, with facilities for handling conventional cargo, particularly forest products, as well as containers and bulk grain shipments. By then, however, other UK ports, particularly those not in the National Dock Labour Scheme, had taken over Tilbury's role as the leading container port in the country. The burden of the National Dock Labour Scheme and the continuation of other inefficient working practices placed Tilbury at a serious competitive disadvantage.

There had been plans to develop a new integrated port complex on a much grander scale. In 1969 the PLA, mainly thanks to the vision of a future Director General, John Lunch, had been the driving force behind proposals to reclaim 46 acres (19 hectares) from the sea at Maplin Sands, close to Southend, as a major deep-water container port. This was a bold and practical project, technically challenging but wrecked by political considerations, tied in as it was with plans for a third London airport. By the time the government decided to abandon plans for the airport in July 1974, the PLA had taken the decision to concentrate resources on Tilbury.

As cargo-handling methods changed, and the older docks and riverside wharves closed, the problem of surplus labour increased. The consequences of this not only made the Port uncompetitive, they crippled the PLA financially. By 1967, there were 3,000 dockers surplus to requirements in the Port every day who were each guaranteed a weekly wage. Matters were made worse by the introduction of the second phase of the Devlin recommendations in 1970. Productivity deteriorated after the abolition of piece-work rates in return for a higher weekly wage. Bonuses had to be reintroduced in 1975. Port trade declined, falling from more than 60 million tons in 1967 to less than 42 million in 1982. More and more Port employers went out of business. Between September 1967 and September 1976, 159 employers failed, with the loss of nearly 10,000 jobs. From 1968 onwards the PLA was compelled to take over several ailing stevedoring firms just to ensure there were enough stevedores to handle existing trade. Ultimately, the PLA, as employer of last resort under the Scheme, had to take on many of the men from these businesses.

The Authority's position was not helped by the abolition of the Temporarily Unemployed Register. This was achieved under the Aldington-Jones agreement of

The tenure of Lord Aldington, PLA Chairman from 1970 to 1977, was marked by the financial problems created by the accelerating decline of the older docks and the costly severance schemes to reduce the number of surplus dockers employed by the PLA.

Sir John Cuckney, later Lord Cuckney, a leading businessman
and Chairman of the PLA from 1977 to 1979,
recognised the severity of the problems facing the PLA.

Victor Paige, PLA Chairman from 1980 to 1984,
another successful businessman like his predecessor,
was also the son of a docker.

1973, named after the Chairman of the PLA, Lord Aldington, the successor to Lord Simon, and the union leader, Jack Jones. Their agreement led to the allocation of men from the Register to regular employers already struggling to find work for their existing workforce. In the decade after 1975, the Authority absorbed 2,500 registered dockers from other employers. By the end of the 1970s, the PLA was employing more than five-sixths of all registered dock labour in the enclosed docks.

Since it was not possible under the Scheme to make compulsory redundancies, the PLA introduced the first voluntary severance scheme in 1966. Not only was voluntary severance costly, it also attracted more younger

men than older men. The latter, after years of hard work in the docks, were much less physically fit and the PLA found the sickness rate among its workforce rose alarmingly. In the summer of 1977, as John Black was appointed to succeed John Lunch in running an organisation that still employed more than 9,500 staff, over 4,800 of them registered labour, he found that 11 per cent of men working in the enclosed docks were absent through illness.

To accelerate the departure of surplus dockers, severance schemes became increasingly generous. From 1978, the PLA received government assistance towards these schemes in the form of grants, although these later became 'repayable grants'. At the same time the Author-

Sir Brian Kellett, chaired the PLA from 1984 to 1992, tackling the problems left over from the decline of the docks and preparing the Authority for its post-Tilbury future. He is seen here laying the foundation stone for London River House in Gravesend on 18 June 1991, which became the PLA's new administrative centre.

ity was bearing the daily costs of employing men for whom there was no work. The financial burden of all this, coupled with declining revenue from less trade, was devastating for the Authority. The visiting chairman of an Australian port summed all this up very succinctly: 'It sounds to me as if the PLA is like a cow which everyone wants to milk and no one wants to feed.' In 1977 Sir John Cuckney, the PLA's new Chairman, confessed that the Authority was effectively insolvent. Cuckney and his successors during this period, Victor Paige and Sir Brian Kellett, were a different breed of chairmen. They were all successful businessmen: Cuckney chaired a range of major companies, from Westland to Royal Insurance; Paige came

to the PLA from running the National Freight Corporation and would move on to become Chief Executive of the National Health Service; and Kellett spent many years running Tube Investments. They reflected a political consensus for greater commercial drive within the PLA. It must have been a thankless task. As Victor Paige noted in 1980, 'The PLA is no place for the faint-hearted.'

The PLA was not alone in its financial problems. The Mersey Docks & Harbour Board actually declared itself bankrupt. By 1983, the annual cost of surplus labour to the PLA amounted to £5 million (£12 million in today's prices). Requests to write off the PLA's debts were rejected although some limited relief was given under the Ports

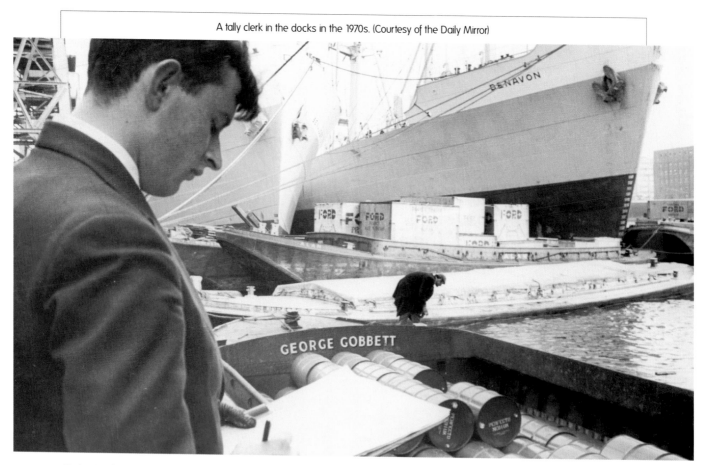

A tally clerk in the docks in the 1970s. (Courtesy of the Daily Mirror)

(Debt Reduction) Act, 1983. In 1984 the government also insisted on reducing Port rates by 30 per cent, at a cost to the PLA of £4 million a year. This followed an objection from the wharfingers who were also suffering badly. The National Dock Labour Scheme, draining money away from the PLA and other Scheme ports, remained unreformed. The reason was easy to see: the dockers remained a mighty force, capable of bringing national commerce to a halt, as they had shown during the month-long national dock strike in the summer of 1972. Resistance to modernisation persisted throughout the 1970s and 1980s, with repeated stoppages, such as the eight-week-long dockers' strike, followed by a three-week strike by tally clerks, in 1983. The government shrewdly

waited to tackle the National Dock Labour Scheme until significant reforms to trades union legislation had taken effect. Norman Fowler was the minister who finally decided the time had come to abolish the Scheme and by the time this was done in 1989 there was little appetite for a fight amongst the remaining dockers. The wait had been costly for the PLA, which had absorbed further irrecoverable costs of more than £26 million (£47 million in today's prices).

The reduction in the number of registered dock workers between 1966 and 1989 had been dramatic, falling from 24,000 in 1966 to 17,000 in 1970 and 9,000 in 1989. The PLA's own workforce declined to 3,245 by the end of 1984 and the last of the surplus dockers left the

34 Berth at Tilbury, seen here in later years, was opened in
response to changes in the way cargo was handled, in this case specifically for packaged timber.

PLA in 1986. One year after the abolition of the Scheme, the PLA was employing fewer than 1,500 people, more than half of them at Tilbury.

Part of the cost of reducing the workforce had come from funds raised through the sale of surplus PLA property. These proceeds had also helped to finance the modernisation of Tilbury Docks. Yet the PLA was never able to maximise the value of the land available for redevelopment after the docks were closed. Firstly, in a rising market, sales were carried out in an unsatisfactory piecemeal fashion. Then, by the time the Authority was showing a more commercial approach through the formation of a development subsidiary in 1973, the property market crashed. There were few bidders for land during

the rest of the decade, although some property was sold off to local authorities. As the market recovered, the aspirations of the Authority were again denied. The government realised that the property portfolio belonging to the PLA (and the public utilities) presented a unique opportunity for the fusion of private enterprise and urban regeneration, and the London Docklands Development Corporation (LDDC) was formed in 1981. The PLA vacated the last of its dockland bases between 1984 and 1986. At the same time, the PLA formed another property subsidiary, Port of London Properties (POLP), in 1984. Under the direction of Jeff Jenkinson, POLP masterminded a series of small housing and industrial developments. Land was developed at the King George V and Royal

The opening of this modern container berth, No.39, at Tilbury, seen here in the 1970s with OCL containers being discharged, was delayed by a year because of industrial action taken by the dockers, causing incalculable damage to the reputation of the Port as it strove to meet the challenges of the cargo handling revolution.

Albert Dock for the City Airport, where the first flight took off in 1987. In the meantime, the LDDC gave the go-ahead for Canary Wharf, the most iconic Docklands development of all, sited at the former West India Docks. Tilbury won the contract to ship construction materials by barge up-river to the site, where the first phase of development was completed in 1991, just as the major phase of POLP's own operations was coming to an end.

On the river the reliable service for users from the PLA's marine personnel contrasted with the disruption caused by the closure of the upper docks and the shift of much commercial shipping downstream. In 1974 the PLA's overall responsibility for pollution control on the river was transferred to Thames Water. The GLC took over the river piers managed by the Authority in 1974, they later transferred to Thames Water before being returned to the PLA

in 1989. In the previous year, the PLA had become responsible for marine pilots, more than eight decades after this had first been suggested. The tragic event of 1989 was the sinking of the *Marchioness* pleasure boat that summer. As well as direct involvement in the aftermath of the accident, the PLA had an important role in coordinating the implementation of the immediate safety improvements.

In the same year the abolition of the Dock Labour Scheme transformed Tilbury's profitability. Within a year Tilbury had moved from a loss of more than £4 million to a profit of just under £4 million (£6.5 million in today's prices). The PLA recognised Tilbury's independence and separated the River Division from the port, transferring the marine services and marine engineering departments in 1990 to new premises at Denton Wharf on the opposite bank of the river. Three divisions – Tilbury, River and

Property – came under the management of three separate chief executives. At the same time a new headquarters was planned at Gravesend, next to the control station for the Thames Navigation Service.

For the PLA, now freed from its financial obligations towards the dockers, Tilbury was an anomaly, the only remaining publicly managed port facility along the Thames. While Tilbury represented a valuable asset, which could be used to repay the outstanding debts to the government, the PLA was in no position to afford the massive future investment required by the port. So the Board, with government support, sought to pilot a private Bill for the privatisation of Tilbury through Parliament in 1990. This proved impossible because of technical problems, but the government, which had been intending to privatise the UK's remaining trust ports, passed a general enabling Bill covering all the major trust ports. An exception was made in the case of the PLA, in that the Bill (which became the Ports Act, 1991) mandated the privatisation only of Tilbury and protected all other aspects of the PLA's work. This approach was taken because the PLA, as a result of the transfer of powers from the Thames Conservancy, was unique among the 50 or so trust ports in the UK in having responsibility for 95 miles of a major river. A competitive bid by Tilbury's management, led by Alan Ravenscroft and John McNab, proved successful and in 1992 the PLA handed over the last of the docks it had taken over in 1909. At a stroke this completely changed the Authority as for the first time in more than 80 years the main focus of its responsibilities became the river itself.

Tilbury became one of the UK's principal container ports.

Shipping in the Pool, by Dora Meeson, 1930.

3 RIVER AND DOCKS

RIVER

With a primary duty to improve and conserve the Thames, the PLA has three key responsibilities – firstly, to facilitate the safety of all those who use the tidal Thames; secondly, to help to conserve the marine environment; and thirdly, to promote the commercial use of the tidal Thames. These objectives cover almost everything that occurs on the river. As far as safety is concerned, the PLA regulates river traffic, maintains shipping channels, provides a pilotage service and supervises sporting and other major events on the river. In relation to the marine environment, the Authority, which once had overall responsibility for the control of river pollution, is still involved in keeping the river free from driftwood and oil spillages. The PLA is also the licensing authority for all structures that go under, cross over or are on the river. Throughout the PLA's history, the wharves and terminals along the river have played an important economic role in the development of the Port. Today the PLA helps to sustain and develop the commercial use of the Thames through safeguarding existing commercial riverside sites and by promoting the use of the river for the carriage of freight wherever possible.

Since 1909 boundary changes have altered the length of the river in the PLA's care. Today the PLA looks after 95 miles of the Thames, stretching from just below Teddington Lock downstream to the outer Thames estuary, to a line roughly between Margate and Clacton.

As the river progressively changes character down river, so do the demands made on the PLA. The upper reaches, covering the stretch from Teddington to Putney, are the crucible for much of Britain's finest rowing talent. With some stretches lined by house-boats and smart riverside properties, they are also a pleasure ground

Radar coverage of the Thames began in the 1950s and was steadily extended to cover much of the river. Radar remains an important element of safety on the Thames. This is the radar mast at Clacton.

for walkers and sailors. The nature

its middle reaches, running

The river between Chelsea and

mainly to pleasure boats, passe

While much of the trade and indu

be replaced by the redeveloped do

ing powerhouses of high finance and

cargo handling is found in increasin

down river, from the Isle of Dogs onward

concentration of aggregates handling in

including Tate & Lyle's Silvertown refine

Dagenham operation. In addition, the occa

the moorings owned by the PLA at Tower

nwich.

PLA became the single authority for the

e in managing all this has been the

r. The PLA specified the requirement

m the outset although initially the

f the Authority, Robert Philipson,

In 1911 F Batty filled the newly

perintendent. Only on Batty's

ccessor, Commander Ernest

PLA's first Chief Harbour

Dredging was part of one of the PLA   g.
Seen here with a tug standing

HARBOUR MASTERS

To most Londoners, the Harbour Master's launch patrols represent the public face of the PLA. Interestingly, of all the PLA's traditional responsibilities, it is those of the Harbour Masters which have the most historic roots. From 1799 onwards, the Harbour Masters were responsible for the supervision of the navigation, mooring, movement, loading and discharge of shipping. Other responsibilities included the inspection of moorings and taking depth soundings. Their primary concern was to ensure safe navigation and the prevention of collisions. By 1828, there was one Harbour Master and three Assistants. Their staff undertook day and night patrols in watermen's skiffs.

In 1857, the City's powers over the river passed to the new Thames Conservancy. The Harbour Masters' responsibilities remained the same, although maintaining the width of the navigable channel and controlling paddle-steamer speeds were given higher priority. There were three Harbour Masters, in charge of the Upper (London Bridge to East Greenwich), Middle (East Greenwich to Grays) and Lower (Grays to Yantlet) Districts.

An Assistant Harbour Master waiting to board a tug at a downstream landing stage around 1930. (Linney Collection, Museum in Docklands)

When the PLA was established, the powers and duties of the Harbour Masters remained essentially the same and the requirement to be examined by Trinity House was continued. The PLA Upper Harbour Master's District stretched from Battersea Bridge to Barking Creek, and the Lower Harbour Master's District ran down to the seaward limit. The area above Battersea was under the control of the River Inspector. Although there have since been numerous administrative and other changes, the PLA's Harbour Masters still touch hands with their predecessors. Today, the Chief Harbour Master – Rear Admiral David Snelson – oversees navigational safety, including emergency management.

He is supported by two Harbour Masters (Upper and Lower, dividing at Crossness), three Deputy Harbour Masters (two Upper and one Lower) river inspectors, launch crews and the officers of the Vessel Traffic Service based at Gravesend and the Thames Barrier. In addition there is the support team running the Safety Management System (SMS) under the Harbour Master (SMS).

Harbour patrol service – the Harbour Master's eyes and ears on the river. Photo shows: PLA General Purpose Coxswain, Steve Mordue, on patrol.

Mapping the river is one of the PLA's key responsibilities. This photo shows one of the PLA's marine survey launches in 1947.

Ernest Shankland was regarded as one of the most influential Chief Harbour Masters in the history of the PLA. As an effective administrator, he ensured the Authority knew the location of every mooring along the river and had an up-to-date record of the ownership of every riverside property. He drove forward the dredging programme originally outlined in 1910 and was responsible for the publication of annual tide tables and improved charts. He worked on measures to alleviate the threat of flooding and pollution. Personally involved in the procurement of new craft for the PLA's river fleet, he had overseen the replacement of every single vessel, excepting the yacht *St Katharine*, with new and improved craft by the time of his retirement in 1948. Among these were not only the Authority's famous floating cranes but also the PLA's first marine driftwood collector, acquired in 1948. Held in high regard by his peers, he had an international reputation. This was cemented by his many publications, including *Modern Harbours* (1926) and *Dredging of Harbours & Rivers* (1931).

Shankland was responsible for a team of Assistant Harbour Masters, each covering a particular stretch of the river. In 1929 the Harbour Master for the Upper River was stationed at Tower Pier, London Bridge, and the Harbour Master for the Lower River at Gravesend – a geographical split that, although the office bases have changed, still applies today. They in turn were responsible for a team of inspectors and assistant inspectors, chief boatmen, boatmen and 'boys'. They carried out their duties in launches, motor boats and rowing boats. Their

work was governed by the PLA's bye-laws, which covered everything from the carriage of inflammable substances, such as calcium carbide, to the protection of fisheries. They dealt with barges dropping anchor in prohibited locations, lighters sinking off wharves, steamers masking dock entrances, collisions during fog and ships leaking oil.

The Authority's workboats and inspection launches remain the marshals of the river. They have

PLA hydrographers at work in 1950 fixing the
position of a bucket dredger.

helped to control the flow of river traffic whenever normal routines are disturbed. These can occur through an emergency or major structural alterations, such as the widening of London Bridge in 1965 or the construction of the Thames Flood Barrier between 1974 and 1982. Today the PLA's river fleet of more than 40 vessels, based since 1990 at Denton Wharf, ranges from launches and workboats to sophisticated survey ships. By the turn of the new millennium, the PLA was providing river surveillance around the clock, with continuous harbour service launch patrols downstream from Putney and daylight hours every day upstream.

Enforcing the bye-laws is not always an easy task. It has helped, as *The PLA Monthly* noted in 1962, if the Assistant Harbour Masters were 'personalities to the shipmasters, pilots, tug skippers, watermen, lightermen and frontagers' on their own section of the river. The Chief Harbour Master's duties have increased steadily – in 1996, for instance, he was given overall responsibility for the PLA's marine pilots – but the stamp which Shankland placed on the role has influenced the work of his successors, including latterly Gordon Varney, Bruce Richardson and David Snelson.

The Authority has been tasked with constantly improving safety on the river since its foundation. In the days before modern navigational aids, the PLA instigated a service in 1932 to broadcast weather conditions during fog at Gravesend. This enabled vessels to take the precaution of anchoring further down the river and minimised the usual congestion in Gravesend Reach. One observer, Tom Stothard, born in Blackwall in 1908 and a regular shrimper off Gravesend, recalled the scene at Gravesend on a misty morning. The clearing fog revealed a host of vessels at anchor waiting to move up the river with the tide: 'So, here on the flood tide, large ships, little ships, sailing barges, tugs with crafts behind them, it was an amazing sight.' After the war, the PLA used the Great Nore Tower in the estuary for fog-signalling. This lasted until its partial collapse after being hit by a vessel in 1953, killing the four-man watch-keeping crew.

The variety of ships using the Port reached its peak in the inter-war years, when ocean-going ships made around 50,000 annual visits, coasters around 15,000 trips, and some 300,000 passengers arrived and departed. River craft included 250 tugs, 10,000 lighters and 1,000 sailing barges. In 1938, Frank Bowen listed 53 different types of ships and vessels, including colliers, coasters, North Sea packets, passenger liners, oil tankers, cargo liners, meat carriers and pleasure steamers. Ships sailed to over 300 foreign ports and there were regular steamer services to 36 continental ports. Coastwise services ran to 74 British ports. Most of the 'short sea' continental and coastwise steamers operated from the riverside wharves, the London and St Katharine Docks, and Regents Canal Dock. Bigger ships operated from the larger docks. The Greenland Dock was home to the Cunard Line and the Canadian Pacific Steamship Line. Steamers of the Ben Line, Ellerman Wilson Line and

Tilbury was a main port of call for ocean liners well into the 1950s. P&O's *Strathaird*, seen here approaching the entrance lock to the docks in 1949, plied the Australian run. She was launched in 1932, shortly before the shipping company appointed a new Chairman, Lord Craigmyle, who as Lord Justice Shaw had chaired the inquiry into dock labour in 1920.

The *Rangitiki*, of the New Zealand Shipping Company, seen in the Royal Albert Dock in 1955.

Harrison Line used the West India Docks. The Millwall Dock was used by the British & African Steam Navigation Company, Persian Gulf Line and the Swedish Lloyd Line. The Ben Line, Blue Star Line, Ellerman Lines, Lamport & Holt Lines and the Union Castle Line used the East India Docks. The Royal Docks berthed ships of the Blue Star Line, British India Steam Navigation Company, Cunard Line, Donaldson Line, Houlder Brothers Line, New Zealand Shipping Company, Peninsular & Oriental Steam Navigation Company, Royal Mail Line and Shaw Savill & Albion Line. The main lines using Tilbury included Bibby Line, Clan Line, Ellerman Lines, Harrison Line, Orient Line and the Peninsular & Oriental Steam Navigation Company. The port had 28 graving docks for ship-repairing. The Thames bridges, parks, public piers and pleasure steamers attracted thousands of spectators who came to see the ever-changing vista of the 'City of Ships'.

The *City of Pretoria*, proceeding to her berth with the assistance of tugs in the West India Docks in 1962, was among the larger vessels seen in the docks in the early 1960s.

Technology became more sophisticated as a result of developments stimulated by the war. The PLA introduced short-wave radio in 1948. Radar was installed for the first time in 1955, on board the PLA vessel *Yantlet*. Four years later, the PLA established the Thames Navigation Service (TNS), based on VHF radio and harbour surveillance radar, with staff led by master mariners. Two PLA Harbour Service launches were also equipped with radar, allowing patrols to be maintained in poor visibility.

At the time just one per cent of vessels using the river were equipped with VHF radio. By 1963, more than half the ships entering the Pool of London had adopted the system, benefiting from the work of the TNS. At first, radar covered only Gravesend Reach but between 1959 and 1965 the TNS extended radar coverage over 51 miles of the river. By 1968 it was possible to monitor shipping all the way from Southend to Erith, and by the 1980s to Greenwich.

Another innovation was initiated in 1964 when the Authority set up a network of weather report stations and tide gauges from Tower Pier to Southend. This was the first of its kind in the country, reporting to the London Weather Centre every three hours. In 1966 an emergency traffic control system introduced during the national seamen's strike proved so effective in relieving congestion that it was retained as the Shipping Control Centre.

Accidents still occurred on the busy river but the PLA worked constantly to make sure there were fewer of them. Part of this strategy included being the first port authority to seek and secure powers to issue General Directions. The first such direction issued, in 1969, required advance notice of the arrival and departure of vessels, designation of anchorages, compliance with a movement programme and use of the most appropriate approach channel. In 1982, the Authority set up the River Users' Liaison Group as a forum for the discussion of safety

The Thames Navigation Service (TNS), established in 1959, was a major step forward in river safety.
This is the TNS operations room at Gravesend in 1963.

issues. Traffic controls on the river were rigorously enforced. The work of the TNS was constantly upgraded. In 1984 the Port of London River Information System (POLARIS), a vessel data-management system linked with a modern radar display system, was launched, and in 1986 the vessel traffic management system (VTS) became operational.

In spite of all these measures, it is impossible to eradicate all risks on the river. The one major disaster on the Thames since the PLA was established came on the night of 20 August 1989, when the passenger vessel, *Marchioness*, collided with the dredger, *Bowbelle*, and sank with the loss of 51 lives. The tragedy shook public confidence in travel on the river. It was the worst peace-time loss of life on the river since the sinking of the

Princess Alice with the loss of more than 640 lives in 1878. When the *Marchioness* sank, a major incident was immediately declared under the direction of the police emergency management centre at New Scotland Yard. The PLA's Marine Services Manager, Captain Derek Roberts, organised and supervised on scene salvage operations while the Harbour Master Gordon Varney maintained overall coordination of the incident and was responsible for directing other river traffic. The PLA's salvage and diving teams, working in difficult conditions, located, recovered and placed the wreck ashore within 15 hours of the accident. Every member of the PLA staff involved during that terrible time made an outstanding contribution. The navigational safety measures subsequently announced by the government were implemented through the PLA, in

consultation with vessel operators on the river. An investigation conducted by the Marine Accident Investigation Branch, part of the Department of Transport, resulted in the installation of a new system of automatic warning lights. In 1992 these were fitted by the PLA to 19 bridges between Putney and Tower Bridge. Demands for a public inquiry were rejected by the government at the time and it was more than a decade before one took place. The Thames Safety Inquiry, followed by the Formal Investigation into the sinking of the *Marchioness*, both conducted by Lord Justice Clarke, covered not just the circumstances of the disaster but also conducted a wider review of river safety. Reporting in 1999, the Thames Safety Inquiry found most of the criticisms of the PLA unfounded and applauded the work done by the PLA to improve safety. There was one

issue over which the Authority was taken to task. In 2001 the Marchioness Formal Investigation held that the PLA should have issued a formal direction requiring vessels with limited forward visibility to station lookouts on their forecastles, equipped with means of communicating effectively with their wheelhouses. Although a formal direction had not been issued, the PLA had secured an undertaking from the owners of the *Bowbelle* to do just that but it had never been implemented. But the Investigation did not believe that the failure to issue a formal direction had anything to do with the accident. That, it concluded, was caused by the failure of both masters to observe regulation and keep proper lookouts.

A PLA radar tracking ship movements on the river.

The busy river, from Tower Bridge to the Royal Docks, photographed in 1964. Within 17 years, changes in cargo handling would lead to the closure of all of these docks and most of the riverside wharves. (Courtesy of English Heritage)

As navigation and conservancy authority, one of the fundamental roles of the PLA is to make sure there is sufficient water for vessels coming up the river. The PLA's early achievements in this sphere were heavily influenced by the work done by the Thames Conservancy prior to 1909, several of whose members were appointed to the new Authority and whose Secretary, Robert Philipson, became responsible for the Authority's River Division. In particular the Conservancy had commissioned a report from G E W Cruttwell, the engineer responsible for Tower Bridge, who had advocated the dredging of the Princes Channel. Beyond the finances of the Conservancy, this was finally achieved by the PLA in the new millennium. The initial dredging work carried out by the PLA was interrupted by the First World War but resumed with the deepening of two major channels during the 1920s. The dredging of the Yantlet Channel in Sea Reach was finished in 1925, making it 30 feet (9 metres) deep and 1,000 feet (300 metres) wide over 11 miles of the river. A channel similar in depth was completed in 1928, stretching 33 miles from the PLA's seaward boundary to the King George V Dock. In the same year, the PLA took more than

The PLA's very popular river cruises continued well into the 1960s, as shown here, with two packed vessels touring the busy Royal Docks in the summer of 1964.

2.1 million cubic yards of dredgings from the Thames and more than 1.3 million cubic yards from the docks. An integral part of the PLA's dredging operations was its hydrographical expertise. Regular studies of the topography of the seabed are essential in maintaining navigational safety on the river and the reputation of the PLA in this field was forged between the wars.

Dredging was inevitably neglected during the Second World War. From 1945 a more scientific approach to siltation was adopted. As the size of ships using the Thames increased, further major dredging was planned. In 1964, when the seaward boundary of the PLA was extended by 22 miles, work began on dredging the Knock John Channel. Over the next three years the PLA deepened the approach channel to the major oil installa-

tions at Canvey Island, Shell Haven and Coryton. During this period the PLA's hydrographic section used transit sonar equipment for the first time to study the topography of the sea bed. The new channel was opened to shipping in June 1967. The benefits were soon evident. In October 1968, the previous record for the largest tanker to enter the Port (the *Seven Skies*, 93,000 tons deadweight and 286 metres long) was surpassed by the 206,000 tons deadweight, 355 metre long *Megara*.

A further 40 years elapsed before another scheme was undertaken on the same scale. By then, the PLA had ceased to carry out its own dredging, which was sub-contracted from 1991. Supported by the formidable expertise of the PLA's hydrography team, using specialist vessels, the deepening of the six-mile-long Princes

A constant since its creation has been PLA's responsibility for clearing wrecks.
Here PLA salvage vessels raise the *Nova L* from beneath Vauxhall Bridge in January 1978.

Channel was completed in 2008. This created a shorter, quicker southern route through the estuary for all but the largest ships. Today, in any one year, the PLA will typically oversee the dredging of 200,000 cubic metres of material from the river. More than 150 hydrographic surveys will also be carried out. These usually comprise surveys of specific areas of the main river and estuary, combined with regular surveys of shipping berths and the river's constantly changing shoals and channels. The work of the PLA's Port Hydrographer and his team of surveyors has a national and international reputation.

As well as dredging the river, the Authority also keeps the Thames clear of wrecks. In 1928, for instance, the PLA raised 47 sailing vessels and barges, three steam tugs, two small craft and one steamer of 181 tons. Between 1940 and 1950 the department removed 35 ships and 598 small craft from the Thames. In 1965, when the PLA operated a fleet of 20 salvage vessels, staff assisted in the largest peacetime salvage operation yet performed in the Port, the rescue of the MV *Magdeburg*, stranded off Broadness Point following a collision. Salvage staff have been involved in a string of similar incidents over the years. In October 1997, for instance, a PLA salvage team took part in the recovery of the dredger, *Sand Kite*, after it collided with the Thames Barrier in dense fog. The department has also been involved in other essential work, such as recovering lost anchors, replacing lock gates, maintaining moorings and buoys and carrying out surveys.

Part of the PLA salvage team attends the scene of the collision of the *Sand Kite* with the Thames Barrier in 1997.

THE PLA FLEET

On its foundation, the PLA took over a large fleet of vessels from its predecessor dock companies, the London Grain Elevator Company and the Thames Conservancy. These included watermen's skiffs, launches, tugs, lighters, salvage craft, floating steam cranes, floating pneumatic grain elevators, steam dredgers and hopper barges for removing dredged spoil. Amongst the 28 inherited tugs were two paddle tugs – the *Dreadnought* (1867) and *Victoria* (1876) – which were quickly disposed of. New ship-handling tugs, including the *Beam*, *Beverley*, *Walbrook* and the *Westbourne*, were soon commissioned. Across its hundred-year history the PLA owned 75 ship-handling and craft tugs. Between 1951 and 1968, all new tugs were given names with a 'PLA' prefix including the ship tugs *Plagal*, *Plangent*, *Plateau* and *Platina*, and the launch tug *Plaudit*. The PLA had also been quick to order new steam bucket dredgers, including *Dredger No. 7* (1911) and the *India* (1911), and steam hopper barges, such as the *Lord Ritchie* (1912). By the 1950s, the PLA had ten dredgers, serviced by four tugs. Another distinctive element in the fleet were the massive floating steam cranes, including the *London Samson*, *London Titan*, *London Ajax* and the *London Mammoth*.

The PLA Harbour Master's launch, *Ranelagh*, departing Tower Pier in 1959.

One of the many vessels operated by the PLA, the tug *Beverley*, with the SS *Morvada* taking tow before passing through the lock into the King George V Dock on 13 September 1931. (Linney Collection, Museum in Docklands)

The last was the largest, being upgraded to a 200-ton lift in 1960. One of the best-known vessels in the fleet was the sleek hydrographic survey launch *Havengore* (1956) which carried Sir Winston Churchill's coffin at his state funeral in 1965 (see painting on page 100). Today, the PLA no longer operates dock tugs, dredgers and floating cranes. Its fleet of over 40 vessels, however, includes working boats, patrol launches, hydrographic survey craft and pilot cutters.

(Right) The PLA's floating cranes handled the heaviest cargoes in the docks - the *London Titan* and *London Ajax* lift a railway coach onto the *Marwarri* in the Royal Albert Dock in 1947.

(Below) *Richmond* – one of two new PLA launches specially designed for the shallower upper river, generates less wash, uses less fuel and gets the crews closer to river users than the boats they replaced.

Divers are a key part of the Authority's salvage staff. Teams of divers were also stationed in the enclosed docks. Roy Jewiss, who trained as a PLA diver in the 1950s, remembered how diving in the Thames, with its tidal stream, was – and still is – possible only an hour before low water and an hour afterwards. With no visibility below a metre or so, the diver, before he began groping around in the darkness, formed a picture in his head of what lay underneath the water. In those days, air was hand-pumped by two or three hands on deck; after the diver had gone down ten metres or so, pumping became more strenuous, and, if the pumpers tired, the diver would start to experience intermittent blackouts. Before modern neoprene suits and other lighter apparatus, diving gear was cumbersome, weighty and inflexible. Heavy boots, tough canvas suits and more than 60 kilogrammes of lead on the breast plate reduced divers to crawling around on their hands and knees when they reached the bottom of the river.

The separate salvage and docks diving teams combined in the early 1970s. Today divers still work regularly in the river, still in zero visibility, carrying out a wide range of activities. In just one year, 2004, PLA divers undertook 158 diving operations, including the inspection of the damaged keel of a large car carrier and the clearance of 11 fouled propellers. Recently they have been

PLA diver Ted Brand preparing for a dive with his linesman in 1949.

instrumental in helping to raise the partial remains of a late sixteenth-century wreck discovered during the deepening of the Princes Channel. They have also been involved in preparatory work for the construction of London Gateway, the major new container terminal planned for the site of the former oil refinery at Shell Haven.

Pilots joined the PLA much more recently. The Royal Commission of 1902 had recommended that any new port authority for London should assume control of the river pilots. More than 80 years later, with a view to improving the efficiency of the service, the government made the same proposal in 1984. The Pilotage Act was passed in 1987 and, in anticipation of this new responsibility, the seaward boundary of the pilotage area was extended to Long Sand Head in 1988. In the same year,

the PLA, along with other UK port authorities, assumed responsibility for navigational buoys, lights and marks, port-dedicated sea pilotage and river pilots. The 300 self-employed pilots, deciding they could no longer afford the insurance risks on the Thames, voted in favour of becoming employees of the PLA. They transferred to the PLA on 1 October 1988. The integration of these skilled and experienced men as employees within the organisation took some time and the PLA's head of personnel management worked hard to secure this. The PLA also took the

A section of a 1937 photographic panorama of the river, commissioned by the PLA, shows Tower Pier, which provided accommodation for the Harbour Master's service, with the PLA's Head Office in the background.

A member of today's PLA
diving team – Michael Russell.

The staff of today's PLA - a pilot boards a vessel.

opportunity to make the service more efficient. After further training, the same pilots were able to take ships from the sea to a number of berths and vice versa; while, within certain criteria under the Pilotage Act, more masters and mates, equipped with the necessary pilotage exemption certificates, were piloting their own vessels. All this helped the PLA to keep down Port operating costs for shipping. Within a few years, as intended by the Act, the efficiency of the service had increased and the number of pilots had been reduced to less than a hundred.

In 1990 the pilotage service was integrated with the TNS within a single Port Control Centre at Gravesend, under the charge of the chief harbour master. The Authority was quick to take advantage of accelerating advances in modern technology. By 1993 GPS (Global Positioning System) on vessels was becoming common place and the electronic charts were starting to be fitted on some vessels, improving their navigational safety. The Port Control Centre was upgraded in 1993, the room layout was remodelled and new equipment installed which included a new radar display tracking system using the latest computer based technology. In 1995, under the Merchant Shipping Act, the PLA also became the local lighthouse authority. In 1996, the first dedicated Emergency Management Centre was established at Gravesend, and the post of Marine Emergency Planning Officer created. The Authority recognised the importance of emergency planning and the need to work closely with the emergency services, local authorities (across three administrative areas) and other agencies likely to be involved in a marine emergency in the Port.

From January 1994, Class 1 pilots have worked regularly as Duty Port Controllers, allowing vessels to take advantage of their extensive knowledge and expertise. Twenty years after becoming part of the PLA, pilots have become a much respected and appreciated part of the Authority. The imminent development of London Gateway will bring many more and larger vessels into the Thames and the PLA's pilots have already shown they are more than competent to meet this challenge – in 2007 the

The river piers were the PLA's responsibility on and off from 1909 until 1999. Here Westminster Pier is being towed downriver on 3 November 1949 for an overhaul in the Surrey Docks.

largest ever container ship to come into the Thames, the 91,560 tonnes, 346 metre long *Sovereign Maersk*, capable of carrying more than 8,050 standard containers, was brought safely into Tilbury.

At the heart of the PLA's work to maintain and promote safety on the river is the Port's navigational Safety Management System (SMS), developed and maintained in compliance with the requirements of the UK's Port Marine Safety Code. Since 2007 the SMS has been complemented by a requirement for specific vessels in the busy central reaches of the river to operate the Thames Automatic Identification System (AIS). While not to be used for navigation, this transponder system allows each vessel carrying it to obtain an overview of vessel traffic in the immediate area. In particular this overcomes the problem in central London where topography and poor sight lines prevent the effective use of radar. The PLA played a major role in developing the application of this technology for the Thames and subsequently supported its introduction finan-

cially, meeting half the cost of the units that had to be fitted to vessels working in central London. Also in 2007, the Maritime and Coastguard Agency introduced the National Boatmaster's Licence. For the first time this required those navigating both passenger and freight vessels on inland waterways throughout the UK to demonstrate their competency. This brought to an end the PLA's responsibility for licensing watermen and lightermen, which had been administered on behalf of the Authority since 1909 by the Company of Watermen and Lightermen.

From time to time throughout its history the PLA has been involved in the management of the piers on the river. In 1909 the LCC handed over 17 piers to the PLA. Passenger traffic along the river was important – in 1912 these piers were used regularly by 214,000 people working on the river – but rarely profitable. The piers were maintained by the PLA at a loss. Passenger services were generally unsuccessful. The LCC's 'penny steamers' lasted just two years, from 1905 to 1907. Proposals for

When travelling on the river, Her Majesty the Queen uses the PLA's launch *Royal Nore*. On these duties, the *Royal Nore* flies the royal standard at the jackstaff. On the most formal occasions, the Queen is accompanied by the Royal Bargemaster along with eight Royal Watermen, in full ceremonial dress, standing on the fore deck.

another service during the 1930s came to nothing. After the success of the emergency passenger service run during the war, the Thames Waterbus Service ran a successful pilot scheme from late July to late October 1947. Although this carried nearly 470,000 passengers, it was discontinued at the end of the trial period. Another limited service was run during the Festival of Britain in 1951–52. The PLA encouraged further attempts but all these came to nothing. The reasons for the patchy success of passenger services on the Thames include the serpentine course of the river and the uneven distribution of the piers. This means a journey by water sometimes takes longer than other forms of public transport. Yet passenger services on the river are probably more successful today than they have ever been. The recent expansion of the Thames Clipper operation to offer services every 15 minutes is founded in part on significant investment in the leisure attractions at the former Millennium Dome, now the O_2.

River cruises have always been popular. For many years the PLA ran its own summer cruises down-river from Tower Pier and around the docks. Cruises for invalid soldiers had been organised during the First World War but it was not until 1931 that the PLA began cruises for the general public. Suspended on the outbreak of the Second World War, they were revived in 1949 and were still running in 1965. In 1963, 23,000 passengers were carried on 63 outings. Today catamaran hulled vessels predominate in this market.

Over the years the PLA removed a number of piers, added others and improved the remainder. In 1951 the PLA took on the Festival Piers created by the LCC for the Festival of Britain. Several major piers, including the Lower Tower Pier, Charing Cross and Westminster, were handed back to the LCC's successor, the GLC, in 1974. They were then passed to Thames Water on the abolition of the GLC 12 years later and back to the PLA after the privatisation of the water companies in 1989.

By then, the cash-strapped PLA needed the piers to pay their way but also wanted them to be used more efficiently. Focusing increasingly on the river as Tilbury was prepared for privatisation, the PLA consulted pleasure-boat operators before making wider changes. In 1992, as a result, the boat operators gained longer contracts and fixed slots for the use of the piers. In return they agreed to keep their boats well maintained and improve facilities on board.

In 1996 the PLA sold five smaller upstream piers to the private sector. The Authority also embarked on a plan for upgrading the piers in central London. Charing Cross Pier (now Embankment Pier) was completed to a radical new design in 1998, followed by the rebuilding of Tower Pier, again to a new design, begun in 1999. The PLA drew up similar plans for Westminster and Bankside Piers, but the piers had been transferred to another body yet again before these works could be carried out. The new organisation, London River Services, part of Transport for London, assumed control of the piers at Westminster, Embankment, Festival, Tower and Greenwich in 1999, in advance of the formation of the Greater London Authority (GLA). Today the PLA owns just three piers, Royal Terrace Pier at Gravesend, Denton Wharf and Barrier Gardens Pier. The last was recently acquired as the Authority's operational base for the Middle District, adjacent to the PLA's existing Thames Barrier Navigational Control centre.

State ceremonials and other public events on the river fall under the supervision of the PLA. These are often complex events with inevitable implications for other traffic using the river and require considerable advance planning. The Silver Jubilees of 1935 and 1977, the Coronations of 1937 and 1953 and the Golden Jubilee of 2002 were all celebrated on the river. For the Silver Jubilee of George V in 1935, the stretch of river between the Upper Pool and Lambeth Reach was renamed King's Reach. In 1977 the PLA organised a river pageant as part of the festivities for the Queen's Silver Jubilee.

In 1970, the PLA instructed the build of a new 'port inspection launch', which should act as the royal barge for such events. Commissioned in 1971 as the *Nore*, Her Majesty commanded that the vessel should be renamed *Royal Nore* in 1978, in recognition of this important role and most notably the success of the Silver Jubilee celebrations. In 2006-7, *Royal Nore* was rebuilt, receiving new engines and machinery and other major improvements reflecting the best of contemporary British design and manufacture. This work has prepared the launch to continue her central role in state, ceremonial and other high-profile public events.

SPORT ON THE RIVER

As navigation authority, the PLA regulates and supervises sporting and other events on the river. From the Thames Conservancy, it inherited the power to hold regattas on the river. As *The PLA Monthly* noted in 1963, 'the rights of sportsmen using the Thames are respected by the PLA, and it is to the PLA that they turn for help, care and protection'. The PLA has overseen the arrangements for the annual Oxford and Cambridge Boat Race, inextricably linked with the Thames, since the Authority was created. Under the direction of the PLA's Harbour Master for the Upper River, careful planning and preparation are carried out, from contacting all the emergency services well in advance to checking the course the week before and ensuring the river is free from debris. In 2006 the growing popularity of rowing, combined with the increased recreational use of the river, led the PLA, in consultation with recreational users, rowers, sailors, canoeists and others, to introduce a Code of Practice

for Rowing. Devised jointly by the PLA and the Thames Regional Rowing Council, this was backed by financial prizes for rowing clubs demonstrating the keenest commitment to enhancing safety.

Every year the PLA is involved with the authorisation and coordination of more than 50 major events on the river. One is the annual Doggett's Coat and Badge Wager race, which in 1997 was won for the first time by a PLA employee, apprentice Michael Russell. Others have included the 'Transport On Water' Barge Driving Race and the Great River Race. The former, begun in 1975, involves several teams driving 30-ton barges over a course between Greenwich and Westminster Bridge. Commemorating the skill of the lightermen, the race also draws attention to the continuing importance of the river for the movement of freight. The Great River Race, which took place for the twentieth time in 2008, covers an even longer course, stretching 22 miles from Richmond to Greenwich. With up to 300 traditional boats, from wherries to watermen's cutters, taking part, the winners become the UK Traditional Boat Champions.

The Head of the River Race, March 2008, one of the many sporting events supervised by the PLA.

Rowers on the river at Putney.

The Thames has always been the focus of important state occasions. One of the most moving of these was the state funeral of Sir Winston Churchill on 30 January 1965, captured here on canvas in *Westward to Blaydon* by Wilfred Morden.

One of the most touching ceremonies organised by the PLA was the final part of the state funeral for Sir Winston Churchill on 30 January 1965. Churchill's links with the Authority dated from its inception, which he had overseen as President of the Board of Trade in 1909, and were strengthened during the dark days of the Blitz in the Second World War. The Authority bade its final farewell by bearing Churchill's coffin on board the PLA launch, *Haven-gore*, from Tower Pier to Festival Pier. The cranes along Hays Wharf famously lowered their jibs in respect. 'Nothing that could be done to enhance the grandeur and solemnity of the occasion was left undone,' recorded *The PLA Monthly*.

More recently, almost every member of staff employed by the PLA was involved in the two years of planning for the celebration on the river of the advent of the new Millennium on New Year's Eve 1999, with its river-based firework display.

While concern about the conservation of the natural environment has increased in recent years, the PLA has been at the forefront of improving the condition of the Thames for the last hundred years. The state of the river in 1909 was still poor – the water was black and full of rubbish, while untreated sewage from storm-water culverts took 80 days to travel from London Bridge to the sea. The Metropolitan Board of Works had introduced 'sludge boats' disposing of sewage at sea, and they continued to operate from Beckton and Crossness until 1998. But the run-off from storm-water culverts was a problem largely ignored until the recent ambitious Thames Tideway proposal. During the inter-war years the condition of the river deteriorated. In 1923 the lower reaches were described by the Corporation of the City of London, the public health authority for the port, as filthy and stinking, polluted by ineffectively treated sewage and discharges from riverside power stations and gas works. The serious floods of January 1928, with their inevitable impact on river pollution, prompted the PLA to establish a pollution committee. In liaison with other interested parties, notably local authorities, the public utilities and the river boards, the PLA was influential in persuading local councils to improve the way they disposed of sewage and in negotiating agreements with new power stations to modify their discharges. The work of the PLA helped to establish new standards for the level of effluent discharged into the river. During the 1930s the PLA also adopted a scheme for carrying out a chemical and biological survey of the river, accumulating over several years the necessary evidence to promote further measures to improve river quality.

Unsurprisingly, sewage pollution worsened during the war, and once peace returned the PLA continued to press the LCC, and government, for action. Complaints from river users about the appalling state of the river continued to multiply during the 1950s. The pollution could turn the sparkling brasswork of a ship purple between Gravesend and Woolwich. Diver Roy Jewiss recalled that 'the water used to be a horrible mauvy blue colour, black, like you can't describe it really, it was foul.' Pollution from sewage and heated cooling water was at its worst and the PLA was concerned that this,

combined with water extraction, was accelerating the silting up of the river.

The LCC drew up a ten-year programme of improvements. This was supported by the government, which also passed the Rivers (Prevention of Pollution) Act, 1951, and the Clean Air Act, 1957. The PLA also imposed more stringent conditions to ensure a suitable standard for the cooling water returned to the river from the new power stations built after the war. These included Bankside, Brunswick Wharf (built on the site of the filled-in East India Export Dock), Belvedere and Tilbury. At the same time, many of the noxious gas works closed down.

All this joint action gradually began to make an impact on the level of pollution, which halved during the 1960s. Through the Port of London Act, 1964, the PLA gained control over the discharge of all trade effluents into the river. Through its Pollution Control Committee, set up

From 1909 until 1974 the PLA was responsible for monitoring river pollution. Here River Purification Officer Leonard Betts squelches through mud at low tide to take samples from exposed outfalls in 1950.

Scientists on board the PLA launch *Shornmead,* determining levels of oxygen in the Thames in 1954 when the condition of the river was still poor. (Crown Copyright)

salmon were being reintroduced. In 1973 the PLA established the Port of London Salmon Trophy. Although several salmon were removed from the river during the 1970s, the trophy was not claimed until 1983. Ten years later, in July 1993 Paul Collins landed a 17-pound salmon at Teddington Weir, the heaviest caught by rod and line in 160 years.

Although the PLA handed over responsibility for pollution control to Thames Water in 1974, under the Water Act, 1973, the PLA has retained an influential voice, formerly through its river committee and currently through its licensing regime, lending support to further initiatives for improvement.

The influence of the Authority was seen in its approach to the periodic flooding that occurred along the Thames. The PLA was not charged with responsibility for the prevention of flooding but it was concerned by the impact of any consequent damage and loss of life. The solution advocated by the Authority's engineers was the creation of a barrier in the estuary at Gravesend. The severe flooding in 1928, which killed 14 people, prompted the PLA to repeat its call for such a barrier and take an active role with other parties in the planning of future flood prevention.

There were very high tides in 1938, 1949 and 1951 but the most disastrous flood occurred on the night of 31 January 1953. There was flooding along the Thames as far upstream as Putney. On Canvey Island, which was completely inundated, 58 people were drowned. Relief operations were based at the PLA's Cutler Street warehouses. The storm surge affected much of the east coast of England, from Hull to Deal, and the death toll exceeded 300. In March 1960 further serious consideration of building a Thames Flood Barrier was revived, with a paper presented to Parliament. The PLA insisted that the only acceptable barrier would be one which also met what the annual report for 1961 described as 'essential navigational requirements'. Another surge in 1965, which reached the top of the river embankment, demonstrated the urgency of the project. During 1974 the PLA carried

under the Act in 1967, the PLA did much to persuade manufacturers to phase out their use of heavy detergents and develop biodegradable alternatives. This was helped by the Authority's more careful use of its licensing and river accommodation duties.

In the ten years following the 1964 Act, the Thames, thanks to the action of the PLA, in partnership with business, government and the riparian boroughs, was the only major industrial river in the world to show any marked improvement in quality. Large flocks of wildfowl, encouraged by cold winters, gathered in the lower Thames. They fed on tubifex worms, although, with the increasing cleanliness of the river, the worms declined and the number of birds diminished. Fish began returning. Previously only eels, able to tolerate high levels of pollution, could flourish. By the early 1970s there were 86 species of freshwater and marine fish in the river and

out preparatory dredging in advance of the start of construction work. Throughout this work, the PLA insisted that safe navigation was maintained at all times. The Thames Flood Barrier began operating in 1982 and was formally opened in 1984.

The PLA had an interest in other aspects of the condition of the river. The Port of London Act, 1968, formalised the work already being done by the Authority to keep the river clear of driftwood and other debris. In 1966, when specialist driftwood collection vessels, the *Gog* and *Magog*, had been commissioned, the PLA was collecting some 5,000 tons every year. From the mid-1970s driftwood clearance was jointly funded by the PLA, Thames Water, the GLC and, later, the riparian boroughs and, for some years, the LDDC. In 1987 business sponsorship was obtained for replacement craft for the first time. These were joined in 1988 by passive driftwood collectors, constructed to the specification of Captain Derek Roberts. With the PLA's support, an additional operation, Thames Clean, was started in 1994. The two organisations combined their services in 1998 to form Thames21, named after Agenda 21, the programme for sustainable development unveiled at the Earth Summit in Rio de Janeiro in 1992. Thames21

was backed by bodies ranging from Thames Water, British Waterways and the Environment Agency to the City Corporation and the Tidy Britain Group (now EnCams).

The PLA, through the provision of craft and staff, remains Thames21's largest single contributor. During 2007–08, the organisation removed from the river more than 2.6 million litres of litter, including at least five guns, two bomb shells from the Second World War, one wedding ring, several washing machines, a number of knives and the usual array of shopping trolleys, bicycles, traffic cones, tyres and plastic bags. Including the litter recovered from tributaries and canals, the volume collected would fill more than 27,000 wheelie bins or one and a quarter Olympic-sized swimming pools.

Handling oil spill pollution remains the PLA's responsibility and in 1993 the Authority developed a pollution response vessel based on a catamaran to fulfil this role. The aptly named *Recover* is equipped with rotating polypropylene brushes that sweep spilt oil from the river surface into holding tanks onboard. During that same

The PLA provides a primary oil spill response on the Thames. This is a spill clearance exercise in 2007.

year the PLA also established the Thames Oil Spillage Clearance Association (TOSCA), funded by contributions from oil industry river users, based on the volume of oil handled by each of them. *Recover* is still in use today and operates from the PLA's base at Denton Wharf, supplemented when the need arises by other PLA resources and support from specialist agencies.

The PLA, as owner of most of the river bed and the foreshore up to the high water mark, is also the licensing authority for any structure erected on, over or under the river. This is an important role since any new works on the river can have an impact on the current, and thus on navigation, out of all proportion to the works involved. Many of the powers assumed by the PLA were inherited from previous bodies, such as the Thames Conservancy and the Corporation of the City of London. The way in which the Authority administered its planning responsibilities, through its Harbour Masters and the river committee, dealing with every sort of structure, from discharge pipes to wharves and buildings, as well as events on the river, influenced Herbert Morrison in devising the Town and Country Planning Act, 1947. To the PLA can be attributed in part the system of planning regulation which still operates throughout the UK.

As licensing authority, the PLA has been involved with all the tunnels and bridges constructed along the river over the last century. Several bridges have been added to the river during the time of the PLA, while others have been rebuilt. The new bridges include those at Twickenham and Chiswick completed in 1933. Among those rebuilt were Lambeth, Southwark, Vauxhall, Waterloo and London bridges. The first new tunnel to be built after the foundation of the Authority was that at Dartford. Although the idea for the tunnel originated in the 1920s, design work began only in 1938, was interrupted by the war, and resumed in 1953, with the completion of the tunnel ten years later. In 1967 the second Blackwall tunnel was finished, followed in 1980 by the second Dartford crossing, another tunnel, and in 1991 by the third Dartford crossing, the Queen Elizabeth II Bridge. The latter is the only new bridge to have been built over the Thames east of Tower Bridge. The Millennium Bridge, opened in 2000, was the only major new structure to have no discernible effect on the river.

The river has become a recognised 'green route' in and out of London. The PLA has done much towards this through its work in supporting a sustainable marine environment in which commerce can flourish. Today millions of tonnes of construction materials for major infrastructure projects make their way up the river. Huge volumes of waste are sent down the Thames for recycling and disposal. Soon some of this material will be diverted to feed the new Waste to Energy plant due to open at Belvedere Wharf. In relation to the environment, the PLA's team of talented specialists and supporting staff are involved in everything from the impact of new developments on the ecology of the river and the recording of ancient wrecks to the most appropriate location at sea for the disposal of sediment dredged from the river. In collaboration with a range of agencies, the PLA is at the leading edge of environmental protection and enhancement.

The promotion of the river's environmental and economic sustainability is one of the key roles of the modern PLA. In years gone by, the Authority, as the operator of the enclosed docks, was a direct competitor of the private docks and wharves along the river. Today the Authority encourages the return to commercial use of disused wharves.

These wharves have been crucial to the everyday life of the capital. In the 1920s it was estimated that there were at least 1,500 public and private working wharves stretching along the Thames between Brentford and Gravesend. Homes, factories and offices depended on the commodities handled at riverside depots and warehouses. Most of these wharves, like the docks, survived two world wars and the depression to enjoy a post-war revival. The bustling commercial activity on the upper river regularly drew a crowd of bystanders along London Bridge well into the 1960s. Many of these wharves were listed in the PLA Handbook of the time,

LONDON'S LARDER

In addition to the dock warehouses, hundreds of public wharves lined the north and south banks of the river. They handled all sorts of valuable commodities, including colonial produce, dairy produce, grain, meat, rubber and general produce.

From the 1840s, many warehouses were rebuilt to take account of the reduction in the number of dutiable goods, the widening of Customs' bonding provisions and the growing volume of Port trade. As early as the 1870s, around 75 per cent of all cargoes entering the enclosed docks were being siphoned off to the riverside wharves by lighters thanks to the 'free water clause'. In addition, many of the larger wharves built deep-water berths for steamers. Free from many of the overheads of dock operators, and with dynamic owners, the wharves became important players in the Port.

The largest business was the Hays Wharf Group. By the 1930s, the group operated all but one of the south-bank wharves between London Bridge and Tower Bridge. These, together with their warehouses above London Bridge, occupied some 3.25 million square feet (990 square metres) of floor space, making it the largest such complex in the world. At the time, Hays Wharf stored three-quarters of London's provisions – bacon, butter, lard, cheese and eggs – which earned it the nickname of 'London's Larder'. Hays Wharf also handled large quantities of tea, coffee, cocoa, canned goods, fresh and dried fruit, and wines and spirits, as well as general cargoes such as rubber and plywood. Exports included machinery, vehicles, chemicals and other manufactured goods. Lighters and continental steamers were handled by the Port's largest concentration of quayside cranes. The group also had its own stevedoring, lighterage and road haulage operations. Changing trade and new methods of cargo handling, however, resulted in the closure of Hays Wharf in December 1969, with the loss of around 1,000 dockworkers' jobs.

The riverside wharves played an important role in the commercial life of the river, especially the storage of imported foodstuffs. This photo, taken around 1930, shows Walbrook Wharf and Golden Heart Wharf, in the City. (Linney Collection, Museum in Docklands)

including Dagenham Dock, Delta Wharf, Metropolitan and New Crane Wharves, Millwall Wharf, Palmer's and Payne's Wharf, Tower Wharf, Hay's Wharf, Morden Wharf, Fisher's and Cumberland Wharves, Columbia Wharf and Carron and Continental Wharf.

A decade later, most of the wharves had gone, forced out of business by the revolution in cargo handling, changing distribution patterns and the burden of the National Dock Labour Scheme. After the closure of Hay's Wharf in 1969, others quickly followed, including New Fresh Wharf in May 1970, Free Trade Wharf in January 1971 and Butler's Wharf in March 1972. Redundant, deserted and derelict throughout most of the 1970s and the 1980s, wharves like these became potential redevelopment sites, just like the disused docks. By the end of the 1980s, Manbré Wharf and Columbia Wharf had been redeveloped for housing, Hay's Wharf formed part of the London Bridge City development and Chamberlain's Wharf had become the site for the private London Bridge Hospital. The examples are almost countless.

The upper and middle reaches of the river were most affected by this change. Downstream, in the lower reaches, many private terminals were flourishing, others were revived and new ones were opened. In the late 1980s and early 1990s, even as the UK economy veered once more from boom to bust, the Purfleet Deep Wharf was re-opened, a new aggregates terminal was built at West Thurrock, a deep-water wharf was added to Tower Wharf at Northfleet and a French steel producer transformed Welbeck Wharf.

The demise of so many private wharves and the inclination of developers to view every site as ripe for residential development alarmed the PLA. As part of its primary duty to improve and conserve the Port, the Authority was under the obligation to maintain a working river. The PLA campaigned vigorously for the protection and return to commercial use of many of the redundant sites. Despite the occasional setback, the Authority's persistence paid off. In collaboration initially with government and later with the new Mayor of London, the PLA developed a policy robust enough to defeat those still eager to turn key commercial sites on the riverside into residential developments. The continuing challenge was identifying commercial users for the protected sites.

The range of trading activities covered by the 70 or more private wharves and terminals that flourish on the river today are scarcely less impressive than those of a century ago, even though the cargoes carried are now often hidden from sight in metal boxes, and the huge ships that bring them make rather fewer journeys. In a nation still reliant upon the sea for the vast majority of its trade, the capital and its hinterland depend upon the river.

Imported coal fuels Tilbury power station and the woodpulp landed at Northfleet is turned into toilet tissue. Thousands of tons of steel are imported through Kierbeck Wharf on Barking Creek and an immense variety of goods comes into the country on trailers using the ro-ro freight routes based at Dartford, Purfleet, Dagenham and Tilbury. There are wharves specialising in grain, rice, sugar, edible oils and fats, fuel oils and lubricants, aviation spirit, bitumen and aggregates. Some of these goods still find their way further up the river, some are used at the wharves and terminals where they are landed, while most of the non-fuel and non-aggregate goods are shipped out to customers by lorries and rail almost as soon as they are discharged. The PLA's warehouses have long gone, but the PLA's services, particularly pilotage and PACE, the PLA administered port information system, continue to be essential to many commercial operators in the Port today.

Brandy barrels being unloaded from the SS *Barina* at Millwall Dock in 19—. The Port remained a hub for international trade during the brief post-war boom.

SEABORNE TRADE

In 1909 the Port relied for most of its trade on the Empire and this remained true until well after the Second World War. Although the Port retains its international connections, trade with the Commonwealth has now been overtaken by trade with the European Community. In its heyday the Port handled an immense range of cargoes from all over the world, particularly in the warehouses operated by the PLA. Today the balance of trade has shifted. Ever since the PLA was formed London has remained the leading port in the UK for cargoes other than fuel, while over the years, with the PLA's encouragement, the imports of oil and other fuels have also grown. London is still among the top two or three UK ports overall. With the imminent development of London Gateway container port, London looks set to regain its position as the UK's premier port.

For most of the twentieth century, the country's most important trading partners were the colonies and dominions of the British Empire. Links with the Empire had been a central concern in the debate over the creation of the Authority in the first place. Between the wars it was the slump in colonial economies which most damaged trade in the Port. Then, in the 1930s, with the rise of Imperial Preference, advantageous terms for imperial trading partners encouraged rising imports, in particular of fresh produce, from all over the British Empire. Even in the 1960s London still took almost all the Australian wool clip, most of its cheese and half of its butter, nearly all its wine exports, three-quarters of all its meat exports, half of all its fresh apples and pears and dried fruits (sultanas, currants, raisins, prunes, apples, peaches, pears and apricots), and almost half of its canned fruits. Millions of muslin-wrapped frozen carcasses of Australian, New Zealand and South African lamb were shipped to London every year, where the dockers called them 'white mice'. East Africa supplied grain, sisal, cotton and tobacco, tea, coffee and sugar. Regular shipments of Jamaican bananas were still arriving in the Royal Albert Dock in the late 1960s, 40 years after the first cargo arrived at East India Dock on board the *Jamaican Producer* on 6 May 1929.

The post-war decline of the Empire, with the independence of former colonies and dominions, began to change all this in favour of closer links with Continental Europe even before the UK's entry into the Common Market on 1 January 1973. This boosted the trade of all the UK's east coast ports as well as London. The entry terms negotiated by the British government did ensure the retention of the Commonwealth Sugar Agreement, enabling Tate & Lyle to continue to invest in the wharves on the Thames serving its Silvertown refinery. But the massive shipments from the southern hemisphere of apples and pears, beef, mutton and lamb, and canned fruit gradually diminished. Instead, in came Greek peaches, Turkish dried fruit, French apples and lamb. Even so, onions, ginger, seedless grapes, wine, rum and canned lager, honey, fruit juice and wool were still arriving from Australia and South Africa at the end of the twentieth century.

'The Authority,' wrote Sir Joseph Broodbank in 1921, 'is the greatest warehousekeeper in the world'; and that remained true until the decline of the traditional docks in the 1960s. The warehouses, which often specialised in storing particular types of cargo, were an olfactory sensation. Lightermen claimed they could find their way round the docks in the fog from the smells of different commodities, such as fruit and spices, skins and

Dockers towards the end of the war in 1918 bulking up 56,670 lbs of war stores tea for the troops.

hide, nuts and oils. The PLA also weighed, checked, graded and sampled the goods it stored.

Perhaps more than any other dock, London Dock was an aromatic paradise, with tea from India, Ceylon and China, beeswax from Africa, Australasia, India and Pakistan, dried fruits and spices, wines, brandy and port, sherry and Madeira wine. One member of the PLA staff, Ian Flanders, who began working amid these heady aromas in the mid-1960s, swears he can still smell them. London Dock was the Port's great warehousing dock, with goods galore lightered up from docks lower down the river – wool, skins, wines and spirits, ivory, spices, rubber, mercury, essential oils, fish oil, gums, drugs, canned fruits and fish, dried fruit and nuts, sugar, coffee, cocoa, paper, bark, hemp and coir yarn, jute, seeds, coconuts, whalebone, canes, tallow, mats, glue, wax and iodine.

An even more stupendous medley of exotic goods was found outside the docks, in the PLA's warehouses at Cutler Street in Houndsditch and Commercial Road. John Masefield, the Poet Laureate, visited Cutler Street in 1914, and, in a poem admittedly not of his best, wrote how:

*'You showed me nutmegs
and nutmeg husks,
Ostrich feathers and elephant tusks …
You showed me,
for a most delightful hour,
The wealth in the world
and London's power.'*

The staves of a hogshead of tobacco being removed before it is weighed at the Royal Victoria Dock,
the heart of the Port's tobacco trade, in 1930.

WAREHOUSE OF THE WORLD

Even before the creation of the PLA, London's dock warehouses were described as the 'Emporium of the World'. Although the PLA's warehouses were hidden behind tall security walls, some observers were able to gain entry and bring descriptions of their contents to outside audiences. Their observations offered the ultimate geography lesson, positioning the warehouses at the centre of a worldwide web of commodity production, distribution and consumption.

Visitors and readers were left reeling by the scale of it all. In the mid-1920s, the PLA warehouses could accommodate over 1,000,000 tons of goods, including 28,000 pipes of wine; 120,000 casks of brandy; 33,000 puncheons of rum; 1,000,000 bales of wool; 125,000 tons of grain; 500,000 carcasses of meat; 35,000 tons of tobacco and 30,000 tons of tea. The Surrey Commercial Docks had 150 acres of sheds and quays devoted to timber storage, as well as 40 acres of water. Hundreds of other commodities added to the rich mix.

Elephant tusks being weighed and checked on the ivory floor at London Docks around 1930.

Three python skins hung up for inspection at Cutler Street in the late 1920s.

Part of the crammed curio floor at Cutler Street about 1910.

The more exotic cargoes were stored at the London Docks, Wapping, and the Cutler Street Town Warehouses, Houndsditch. At the London Docks, the warehouses housed spices, drugs, dried fruit, ivory, wool and rubber, whilst the quays and vaults stored wines, ports and sherries. Cutler Street housed oriental carpets, porcelain, curios, silks, drugs, ostrich feathers, cigars, cigarettes and tea. Tea, transported by rail from Tilbury Dock, was the staple of the Commercial Road Warehouse, Aldgate. Many other dock warehouses handled specialist cargoes, including: shells at St Katharine Dock; sugar and rum at the West India Dock; dairy produce at the Greenland Dock; tobacco at the Royal Victoria Dock; and chilled and frozen meat at both the latter and the Royal Albert Dock. As A G Linney observed, the sights and smells of these buildings really made them 'Wonder Warehouses'.

Two warehousemen swamped in a sea of ostrich feathers on display at Cutler Street between the wars.

The bulk of the trade passing through the Port throughout the twentieth century was made up of more general cargoes, basic commodities like paper and timber, meat, wool and grain, fruit and sugar, tea, coffee and tobacco, oil and gas. In the 1920s, the tobacco trade had long been centred on the north side of the Royal Victoria Dock, where the main road was known as Tobacco Road. There were more than 40 different varieties of tobacco, shipped in hogsheads from America, bales from China and cases from Russia and Turkey. In the early 1960s, 80 per cent of the UK's tea came on fast cargo liners into London, mainly at Tilbury and the Royal Docks, before being transhipped to upstream warehouses. There, PLA staff inspected and repaired the tea chests, removed damaged tea, drew samples and prepared the tea for sale. In July

1970, when the first container full of tea arrived in the Port, all this changed.

Two commodities were shipped in bulk to London for many years before the containerisation of tea. Grain first came in bulk to London from North America, the Baltic, the Black Sea and the River Plate in the late nineteenth century, before the PLA was formed. Millwall Dock's Central Granary, with its innovatory pneumatic elevators, was opened in 1902. By 1913, Millwall handled two-fifths of the grain arriving in London. Grain was also discharged at West India Dock; in the Royal Docks, particularly the Royal Victoria, where three huge concrete flour mills, Premier Mill, Empire Mill and Millennium Mills, stood on the south quay from the 1930s until the docks were closed in the 1980s; and in the Surrey Commercial Docks,

The docks handled fruit from all over the world - (above) bananas are lifted from the hold of a banana boat in the Royal Victoria Dock in 1946 and (opposite) South African oranges are discharged from the *Dunbar Castle* in a transit shed at West India Docks in 1931.

A contrast in cargo handling – (top) Australian apples are landed in the traditional way into trucks at the King George V Dock in 1965 (courtesy of Getty Images); while (bottom) the first experimental container shipment of Australian canned fruit from the *Ballarat* is unloaded in November 1966.

Bags of beet sugar being trucked away from a coaster and
lighters at West Dock, London Dock, in 1920.
Coastal shipping continued to play an important role in
the Port during the inter-war years.

where bucket elevators shifted grain either into seven
huge granaries or into lighters. Cargoes of grain were
also shipped to the riverside wharves. By 1939 nearly
three million tons a year was brought into the Port. The
major change came when the massive bulk grain terminal
was opened at Tilbury in 1969. This became a mainstay of
the Port's business. It was soon handling two million tons
a year, attracting business that would otherwise have
been discharged on the Continent for transhipment to the
UK. After Britain became a member of the EEC in 1973,
the terminal was also able to switch from importing grain
to the storage and export of UK grain surpluses. In 2007
around two million tonnes of grain, from exports of wheat
and barley to imports of maize, soya beans and animal
feed, was shipped along the Thames.

From the late nineteenth century sugar from the
East and West Indies was traditionally sent over in bags.
Each of these could weigh up to three hundredweight
(more than 150 kilogrammes), making back-breaking,
bloody work for the dockers. Most of the sugar came into
West India Dock, at North Quay, where, recalled one PLA

Sugar being mixed in the hopper heads in the North Quay warehouses at West India Dock in 1925. The dockers have wrapped sacking around their legs for protection - the abrasive qualities of sugar made it one of the commodities dockers least liked working with. Sugar remains an important cargo on the Thames today.

employee, Geoff Ennals, 'the overlying smell … was that of fermenting sugar'. Thousands of bags were unloaded, and each one sampled, graded and stored until sold to one of the refineries. The North Quay was known as the 'Blood Hole' or 'Bloody Alley', because the men's hands and necks were rubbed raw by the sticky, abrasive sugar. By 1939, a million tons a year were being imported, with sugar from the Caribbean discharged at the West India Dock, from Mauritius and the East Indies at the East India

Dock, and sugar beet from Europe at the London and St Katharine Docks. Sugar was one of the first cargoes to be handled in bulk after the Second World War. The first bulk cargo arrived from San Domingo in March 1949, the sugar discharged into lighters by grab cranes and sent off to the refinery wharves belonging to Tate & Lyle at Silvertown. The cargo of 5,100 tons was the equivalent of 42,000 bags. The work was scarcely any easier for the dockers, hand-trimming sugar in the hold all day, where

Modern bulk handling of cane sugar at Tate & Lyle's Silvertown facility.

Dockers working in the hold of a refrigerated meat vessel in the Royal Victoria Dock in 1958.
They wore sacking on their feet to provide insulation against the cold.

the heat of the sugar gave off heady fumes, their legs protected by nothing other than old sacks. By the early 1960s, only a few hundred tons of bagged sugar were still stored in the PLA's West India Docks warehouses. Today, with the Silvertown refinery still in operation, sugar remains an important cargo on the Thames, with 1.2 million tonnes of bulk cane sugar imported during 2007, representing all the UK's EU quota for cane sugar.

The meat trade was also important. One of the PLA's earliest priorities was investing £400,000 (£16 million in today's prices) in a modern refrigerated meat sorting store for New Zealand lamb. Before the First World War, meat was discharged at the West India, Royal Victoria, Royal Albert, Surrey Commercial and Tilbury Docks. The

PLA also had two cold stores close to Smithfield Market. New facilities were provided at the Royal Albert Dock after the war. In 1926, another specialised berth, this time for the South American meat trade, was established on the north side of the Tidal Basin at the Royal Victoria Dock. The whole process was mechanised, with the PLA investing heavily in cranes, but the General Strike in 1926 deterred further private investment. This system was not modernised by the PLA until the mid-1960s. By then, it was too late. The volume of meat held in the PLA's old-fashioned cold stores had halved by the early 1960s as the trade moved to other ports. An electronically controlled meat handling berth in the Royal Victoria Dock, designed to handle ships operated by the meat firm, Vestey, opened

Most of the softwood imported into London arrived at the Surrey Commercial Docks. Here stevedores discharge Baltic deal planks into lighters at Albion Dock in 1930.

in 1965. Within a handful of years it proved to be a white elephant as the trade progressively left the Port. By the early 1970s, while the PLA still handled meat imported from South America, little New Zealand lamb entered the UK through London. In a final attempt to persuade Vestey to continue importing meat through London, the PLA took over Vestey's failing stevedoring firm, Thames Stevedoring, in the early 1970s. It was to no avail. Within 18 months the last of the trade was lost to Southampton although today New Zealand lamb is still handled at Tilbury Container Services.

The two docks that dominated the timber trade during the last century were the Surrey Commercial Docks and then Tilbury. The PLA carried out substantial improve-

ments at the Surrey Docks before the Second World War. Much of this work was destroyed during the Blitz and considerable investment was made in restoring most of this capacity once peace had returned. The post-war demand for timber was huge as the nation began rebuilding and adding to its battered housing stock.

By then, signs of change were already visible, as the small, stoutly built steamer bringing timber from the Baltic, loaded down to her marks and listing alarmingly, was replaced by the modern streamlined motor vessel with up-to-date cargo-handling gear. Before 1939 an average timber cargo amounted to 3,500 tons. A typical cargo on board the Swedish vessel, *Gunvall*, in 1928, consisted of 248,000 pieces of timber, stored loose, in

More oil and gas has been shipped up the Thames than any other commodity during the last one hundred years. Shell Haven was one of the earliest refineries along the river. Here the Anglo-Saxon Petroleum Co. tanker, *Auricula*, lies alongside No.2 Jetty in October 1946.

279 different parcels of 107 different sizes, which took from 27 December until 3 January to unload. Piling the timber began on 25 January and lasted until 14 March.

The major change came with the introduction of packaged timber which saw the demise of the deal porter carrying timber around the docks. First seen at Rochester in 1958, this innovation was swiftly adopted. The Port handled its first large consignment of packaged timber in 1963, when the *Crystal Gem* brought in 2,300 standards of western hemlock. By the late 1960s packaged timber accounted for one-third of all UK timber imports. With the Surrey Docks unsuitable for these larger cargoes, Tilbury took over as the premier timber terminal in the Port. Today forest products, from timber to pulp, continue to be significant trades in the Port.

Throughout the existence of the PLA, the Port's greatest cargo by tonnage has been fuel. From oil in

particular, the PLA has derived a major part of its income over the years. We have already seen how Lloyd George ensured that the Authority became the overall regulator for the carriage of petroleum on the river; and how Lord Ritchie, both as Vice-Chairman and then Chairman, was influential in encouraging the development of the trade in the Thames. Deep-water approaches were improved with the oil companies and their terminals in mind. This provision, and the experience of the Port in handling large petroleum tankers, were great advantages when the time came for the Port to adapt to the requirements of ro-ro vessels and modern container vessels.

Oil has always been a vital but potentially dangerous cargo. The first shipment arrived in the Thames with the arrival of 1,329 barrels on board the *Elizabeth Watts* from Philadephia in 1862. The Petroleum Act, 1871, passed following an explosion at Victoria Dock in 1869,

By the 1990s, when this view of the deep water berth at Tilbury Container Services was taken, Tilbury's importance as a container terminal had been well-established. The berth was later extended.

A modern container vessel passing a river buoy on the Thames.

forbade the carriage of petroleum cargoes any further upstream than a special wharf at Thames Haven. Navigation for any petroleum vessel anywhere on the river in fog was also banned. Until the early 1920s the PLA resisted applications for oil tankers to sail any further up the river but permitted moorings for petrol barges at Rainham. The upstream limit was moved to Purfleet where the oil companies built vast storage tanks. Bye-laws governing safety and the carriage of petroleum were revised following loss of life in two incidents, a fire aboard the sailing

barge *Dorcas* in 1920 and an explosion on the barge *Warwick*. Restrictions on the navigation of petroleum vessels at night were lifted during the Second World War, to remove a ready target for the bombers, and they were never re-imposed.

The first oil refineries on the Thames were Shell Haven, opened in 1916, and Coryton, a joint venture between the firms of Cory and London & Thames Oil Wharves, in 1922 but three-quarters of oil imports before 1939 were refined products, with only 2½ million tons of

crude oil imported in 1938. Two years earlier, oil imports had eclipsed coal exports for the first time, emphasising the shift towards oil. But Shell Haven was operating at only half its capacity. This changed dramatically after the war as political instability in the oil-producing areas, particularly the Abadan crisis in 1951, led the major oil companies to transfer most of their refining to consumer nations. This was coupled with a rapid rise in the consumption of oil, particularly as the numbers of vehicles increased on the roads.

The capacity of the UK refining industry soared from 4.9m tons to 77m tons by 1970. At Shell Haven, capacity rose from 0.9m tons in 1948 to 9.1m tons in 1963. It was a trend which benefited not only London but also its rivals, such as Grimsby & Immingham and Milford Haven. It was also financially beneficial for the PLA. By the early 1960s, oil accounted for over 40 per cent by value of all cargoes in the Port of London, a proportion that has remained largely unchanged. The refineries along the river, at Shell Haven and Coryton, along with the nearby

Roll-on roll-off (ro-ro) freight movements are a key part of today's Port. Photo shows two Cobelfret ro-ro vessels close to the QEII Bridge at Dartford..

Isle of Grain, now accounted for 40 per cent of the UK's total annual throughput of crude oil. This changed as oilfields were developed in the North Sea and other refineries were developed further north. By 1988, for instance, the 24 million tonnes of fuel imported through London were outstripped by the 50 million tonnes from the North Sea going through Sullom Voe in the Shetlands and the 30 million tonnes processed by the refineries at Milford Haven. The last major investment in Shell Haven's refining facilities occurred in the early 1990s.

Encouraged by the PLA, the first import cargo of gas to come up the Thames was Liquid Natural Gas (LNG), brought from the Gulf of Mexico by the *Methane Pioneer* in February 1959, and landed at the Regent Oil Company's Canvey Island jetty. Today the Calor Gas Terminal on Canvey Island handles 90,000 tonnes of

Liquefied Petroleum Gas (LPG) every year.

Given the steady increase in refining capacity at established sites along the river, the announcement in 1998 of the closure of one of the largest, at Shell Haven, as part of Shell's rationalisation of its European refineries, came as a shock. This was a prime deep water terminal in the river, with five jetties and two miles of waterfront. The PLA worked hard to secure the continued use of the site for Port trade and played a part in developing the concept for its potential as a major container terminal. Today that vision is coming close to reality with the imminent start on the construction of the London Gateway container port, with the capacity to double trade in the Port. Obtaining government consent for this nationally significant development took the best part of a decade and was confirmed on 30 May 2007.

From the foundation of the PLA in 1909 almost until the new millennium the Port of London, boosted by the growth in the oil trade, was one of the UK's leading ports. While growing fuel imports, as well as the boom in North Sea oil and gas, later boosted the fortunes of ports such as Sullom Voe in the Shetlands, Milford Haven, Grimsby & Immingham, and the Tees ports, London never lost its position as the UK's busiest port for non-fuel cargoes. From 1909 until 1939, the tonnage of vessels using the Port rose from 40 million to 63 million tons, and the Port's share of UK trade increased from 29 per cent to 38 per cent. In the mid-1960s, a third of the nation's trade still passed through London, while its nearest rival, Liverpool, managed only 18 per cent, and Harwich and Felixstowe, still seen as country cousins, chalked up just 3½ per cent, scarcely more than Southampton.

The 1966 seamen's strike and the 1970 dock strike seriously damaged London's reputation and the Port began to struggle. In 1973, as shipowners moved to the non-NDLS ports, London's share of UK trade dropped to less than 18 per cent. Even so, London still handled 57 million tons of cargo in 1973. Less than ten years later, after most of the docks and many of the wharves had closed, with the Authority still struggling to make Tilbury more efficient, the total tonnage of imports and exports through the Port had slumped to less than 42 million tonnes. The subsequent revival was limited by the changing structure of British ports, and London's port trade has hovered around 50 million tonnes of through cargo annually since the late 1980s.

In terms of overall cargo tonnage, London is behind only Grimsby & Immingham as the leading UK port. As the UK's second most important port, London handles 20 per cent more cargo freight than Southampton and more than twice as much as Felixstowe, although the latter handles more than four times as much container freight as London, and Southampton twice as much.

The most exciting and important development in the Port for a generation is the creation of the port complex at London Gateway by DP World. This gives the Port the prospect of doubling the tonnage of annual cargo. Within a few years the Port of London should regain its overall pre-eminent position among UK ports.

A typical discharging scene as the docks neared their post-war peak. This is No.33 Shed in the Royal Albert Dock in 1959.

DOCKS

The enclosed docks dominated the PLA from 1909 until the privatisation of Tilbury in 1992. The PLA invested heavily in the docks from the moment the Authority was formed. Modernisation began before the First World War. Work disrupted by the war was completed during the 1920s and there was some limited mechanisation before 1939. Running the docks was a huge operation, requiring a vast range of plant and machinery. The PLA even had its own railway network. After the destruction caused during the Second World War, the Authority spent ten years reconstructing the docks. This was influenced by mechanisation but the advent of revolutionary methods of cargo handling gradually rendered the upstream docks redundant. Closures began in the late 1960s and ended in the 1980s, with vacant land sold off for redevelopment. At the same time, the Authority concentrated on turning Tilbury into a modern cargo-handling centre. The abolition of the National Dock Labour Scheme in 1989 made possible the sale of Tilbury in 1992 and brought an end to the Authority's direct involvement with the docks after more than 80 years.

The scale of the investment poured into London's docks by the PLA before the First World War was ample justification for the creation of the Authority. The private dock companies had struggled and failed for years to do the same thing. Covering 2,700 acres of land and employing around 12,000 people in 1909, the docks were a huge undertaking. They stretched from the historic St Katharine and London Docks, past the busy jumble of the Surrey Commercial Docks on the south bank and the West India and Millwall Docks, with the East

Representing a major investment by the PLA, the King George V Dock was probably the most up to date dock in the world when it opened on 8 July 1921, the day this picture was taken, showing 42 new Babcock & Wilcox electric cranes on the southern quayside.

A Finnish barque glimpsed through timber stacks at Surrey Commercial Docks in 1926.

An aerial view of the Royal Docks in 1964, the peak
post-1945 year for the Port when more than 61 million tons of
cargo was handled, a record still to be broken.
(Courtesy of English Heritage)

India Import Dock, on the north bank, down to the great expanse of the Royal Docks along the north side of Woolwich Reach, and on to the last of the docks 14 miles downstream at Tilbury. After the opening of the King George V Dock in 1921, the Royal Docks boasted the world's largest continuous stretch of dock water, measuring 244 acres. The Surrey Commercial Docks grew from 380 acres in 1909 to 445 acres by the time they were closed in 1970. Here there were 11 docks, 136 acres of open water and nine miles of quays, with sheds storing 200,000 tons of timber over 58 acres, open storage over another 64 acres, and 70 acres of ponds for floating timber. The wine vaults at the London Dock extended over nearly 28 acres. Tilbury Dock, converted from 450 acres of marshy land in the 1880s, grew to 800 acres by the 1990s.

Every year before the Second World War around 10,000 ships were locked-in to the enclosed docks. The largest vessels were almost always found in the Royal Docks, still regarded in the 1960s, according to *The PLA Monthly*, as 'the showpiece of the Port of London for on any busy day it has a concentration of over 50 large ships'. By then the total PLA estate amounted to 5,000 acres.

On its creation the PLA embarked on the vigorous modernisation of this vast empire, including the construction of new docks and the refurbishment and deepening of existing docks. The First World War brought delays but by

A typical post-war dock scene, showing just how labour-intensive unloading cargo was before the arrival of containerisation. Here the *Beaverdell* is being discharged in the Royal Docks in 1946. (Courtesy of Central Press Photos)

1917 there were imposing new brick and reinforced concrete sheds and improved quays at the London, West India and East India Docks, while at Tilbury the main dock was extended and three new berths were built for the P&O and Orient Lines.

Other parts of the programme were delayed even longer. The King George V Dock, eventually opened in 1921, had been just 18 months away from completion in August 1914. Proposals for a new dock to the north of the Royal Albert Dock, so often debated, were never implemented. The huge tract of land acquired for the purpose remained in PLA ownership until the 1980s.

Throughout the 1920s all the docks benefited from either the completion of works postponed by the war or from new investment. These works were supervised initially by Cyril Kirkpatrick and then by his successors, Asa Binns and Wilfred Shepherd-Barron. At Tilbury a new riverside cargo jetty was completed in 1921, although this proved unpopular with barges because of the river current and tidal fall. A new entrance lock to accommodate bigger vessels, a new dry dock and further extensions to the main dock were finished in 1929.

At the Surrey Commercial Docks, the growth of the softwood trade led to the conversion of three central ponds into the Quebec Dock, opened in 1926, the building of major new sheds in the Russia and Canada Docks, and the deepening of the Lavender and Acorn Ponds, completed in 1931. Rafts of timber, tied together with rope stapled to each log, were still floated in the docks' timber ponds. Some lay there for months, each raft fastened to a pile, their ownership individually identified with T-shaped name boards. By 1939, the Surrey Docks had become the world's biggest timber yard. Works planned during the war for the West India and Millwall Docks were started in 1925. In 1928 the two docks were linked for the first time by a new cutting, which allowed ships heading for the granaries and other berths at Millwall to enter through the South Dock lock two and a half miles further downstream.

In a sign of worsening economic conditions, much of the work at Tilbury and the West India Docks went ahead only with the help of government aid for the relief of unemployment through public works. At the

DOCK BUILDINGS

For most Londoners, dock buildings were secret places, hidden away behind well-guarded dock walls. Between the wars, the PLA's warehouses covered some 500 acres. The Authority had inherited a wide array of warehouses and other buildings, including offices, pumping stations and two hotels, which reflected different functional needs and building styles. The warehouses at Cutler Street, the London and St Katharine Docks, and the West India Import Dock were Georgian. Although these were imposing neo-classical buildings, their form reflected their function as repositories for valuable bonded goods. There was also a large stock of Victorian warehouses, including some at the old upper docks, tobacco warehouses at the Royal Victoria Dock, and sheds at the Millwall, Royal Albert and Tilbury Docks. Most of the docks had replacement, or original, wide-span Victorian quayside transit sheds. Some of the most modern buildings were the frozen meat stores – at the East and West India Docks, and the Royal Docks – and the Central Granary at the Millwall Dock. By 1909, however, much of the building stock was in need of improvement, or replacement. The PLA was quick to adopt the Hennebique system of reinforced concrete construction, which provided immense structural strength, fire resistance and the possibility of more open working spaces. New buildings included two-storey transit sheds at the London and the East and West India Docks (1912–1915), the sheds at the new King George V Dock (1921), Tilbury Cargo Jetty (1921), and cold stores at the Royal Docks (1918 and 1928). After the Second World War, new dock buildings were mostly concrete, or steel, open-span sheds, designed to facilitate mechanised handling. The most significant modern surviving PLA building, however, is the Tilbury Grain Terminal (1969), whose monumental concrete silos are as reflective of the functional tradition as are the surviving Georgian sugar warehouses at West India Quay (1802–1804).

Two of the original West India Dock warehouses and the Dock Office, pictured here in 1955, still survive at North Quay, West India Docks.

A convoy of heavily laden barges leaving King George V Dock in 1948. Lighters and barges were an essential part of the dock system.

same time, in the expectation of similar financial assistance, the PLA planned an ambitious series of works, including road improvements around the docks and an airport sited in the lower reaches of the river. The government was less generous than expected so these works were either scaled down or deferred. The PLA did persuade the LCC to carry out one major road-improvement scheme. Silvertown Way, designed by Rendell, Palmer & Tritton, in which Sir Frederick Palmer was a partner, was completed in 1934. Hundreds of houses were demolished – and new ones built elsewhere – in preparation for the construction in reinforced concrete of the mile-long road. This innovative piece of engineering pioneered the use of grade-separated flying junctions, later to appear in the motorway schemes of the 1960s and 1970s, and is regarded as the first flyover in the UK. With Silvertown Way complete, the PLA next deepened the Royal Victoria and Royal Albert Docks for bigger ships, and reconfigured and improved the north side of the Royal Victoria between 1936 and 1938. New buildings breathed fresh life into the London and St Katharine Docks, the docks closest to the heart of the capital. They were at their busiest between the wars, with as many as 30 ships in both docks, although each vessel was little more than a thousand tons, plus a flotilla of lighters delivering and receiving cargoes.

Passenger vessels were seen frequently in the docks, particularly in the Royal Docks and Tilbury Dock, until the mid-1960s. By 1900 Tilbury was already a major port of embarkation and arrival. The First World War interrupted plans made in 1911 to build a passenger landing stage there and work began only in 1924. With its stylish new terminal building, it was officially opened by the prime minister, Ramsay MacDonald, in May 1930, in front of 650 guests. By then, well over 300,000 passengers were using the Port every year.

In 1939 the *Mauretania*, the largest vessel yet built in the UK, completing only her second voyage by berthing in the King George V Dock, became the biggest ship to dock in the Port. In the same year, from the same dock, Shaw Savill's new liner, the *Dominion Monarch*, left on her maiden voyage, reducing the passage from England to Cape Town to 14 days and to Wellington to 35 days. The larger vessels of another South African line, Union-Castle, such as the *Rhodesia Castle*, also regularly berthed in the King George V Dock, bound monthly for Durban via the Suez Canal. As the Second World War approached, many Jewish immigrants entered Britain through London Dock, often so poor that they could not afford to pay the dock charges for their own possessions.

To operate the docks, the PLA employed a vast range of plant and machinery. The floating cranes in particular were objects of awe. Perhaps the most famous

A red letter day for the Port as tugs assist the 34,000-ton *Mauretania* to enter the entrance lock to the King George V Dock, the largest vessel to do so, on 6 August 1939. The quayside is crowded with people welcoming her after the completion of her maiden voyage to New York.

TRADITIONAL CARGO HANDLING

In the era before the post-war cargo-handling revolution, port work mostly focused on the handling of 'piece cargoes'. These included bags, bales, barrels, casks, chests, crates, sides of frozen meat, rolls of newsprint, hands of bananas, racehorses, zoo animals, vehicles and locomotives. These cargoes were labour intensive – and costly – to work onboard ship, on the quays and in warehouses. Specialised gear and equipment were used to handle these cargoes. Some cargoes, however, came in bulk and were handled more economically. These included grain (discharged by pneumatic gear), phosphates, sugar, coal (discharged by crane grab) and oil (pumped ashore). Onboard

Loose timber being discharged overside in the traditional way in Surrey Commercial Docks in 1963.

ship, gangs of dockers and stevedores worked the piece cargoes out of their hold stows, moved them to the hatchways and prepared them into sets for lifting onto the quay by quay crane, or ship's gear. The PLA docks had some 580 quay cranes. Ships' gear was used to discharge cargoes overside into lighters. On the quayside, goods were trucked to transit sheds and warehouses, where they were weighed, gauged, measured and stowed.

Quayside cranes, barges and lighters are used to discharge the 10,000 ton *Dunbar Castle* at the West India Docks on 13 May 1931. She was sunk during the war in 1940. (Linney Collection, Museum in Docklands)

Goods destined for the upper floors of warehouses were lifted into the 'loopholes' or loading doors by hydraulic wall cranes. Trucking was mostly undertaken by older dockers using sack barrows and hand trucks. Electric platform trucks, however, were introduced from 1920 and came to be used for meat, bags of sugar, hogsheads of tobacco and other cargoes. These trucks, which could also be used in warehouse sheds, eclipsed earlier systems of mechanised conveyors. Other innovations – including ship deck cranes, mobile quay cranes, piling machines, and electric conveyors and gantry cranes – improved cargo handling. These technologies also helped export work, which ended with skilled stevedores stowing hold cargoes safely and efficiently. Essentially, however, the speed of work was still set by men, rather than machines.

Frozen mutton being discharged by conveyor and electric platform trucks in the 1930s at the Royal Docks, which boasted the world's largest frozen meat stores.

Grain being discharged by elevators into barges at the Co-op Mills at Royal Victoria Dock in 1954.

was the *London Mammoth*, built by Cowan & Sheldon in 1926. She weighed a thousand tons and her jib rose 220 feet (67 metres) above the water line. Her original operating capacity of 150 tons was increased to 200 tons in 1960. After sterling service, she was pensioned off in 1975, departing from the Port under tow for Greece. Her replacements, another *London Mammoth* and *London Goliath*, each with a capacity of 250 tons, re-mained in service with the PLA until 1996 and are still in operation with new owners. For many years the extensive railway network run by the PLA was also an indispensable part of the docks.

The *London Mammoth* lifting a railway carriage for export to Nigeria in the busy docks in 1960. (Courtesy of Getty Images)

THE PLA RAILWAYS

Rail has played an important role throughout the history of the PLA, from its early days until the rise of road haulage, as a result of improvements to the road networks, with a latter day renaissance prompted by increasing congestion and environmental concerns.

The dock railways included two passenger lines, the Millwall Extension Railway and the Royal Albert Dock line. The Millwall line ran from Millwall Junction Station via South Dock and Millwall Dock to North Greenwich. Even in 1913 the line, suffering from competition with buses, was in decline. The service was gradually reduced until the line to North Greenwich was abandoned in 1926. On the Royal Albert Dock line trains ran from Fenchurch Street, halting at several PLA stations, including Tidal Basin, Custom House, Connaught Road, Central Station (for the Royal Albert), Manor Way and Galleons. The line never made money and the Blitz brought an end to passenger services in September 1940. At Tilbury, rail links were critical to the success of the passenger terminal and were one of the main reasons for investment in the new passenger landing stage opened in 1930.

The cargo side of the PLA's operation was far more successful. One weakness of the old dock companies was that they could not make the most of rail for onward cargoes because they were unable to secure all the necessary links with the main lines. The PLA succeeded where the private dock companies had failed, improving significantly the efficiency of transferring cargoes. In the 1930s, the PLA had 140 miles of permanent way and 40 steam locomotives, which carried 120 train-loads of wagons every day. The three rail-oriented dock systems – West India and Millwall, the Royals and Tilbury – had their own 'exchange sidings', where PLA locomotives took over wagons from the railway companies. The largest was the Exchange Sidings at the Royal Victoria Docks, which also served as the headquarters of the PLA Railway

A train leaving Exchange Sidings, North Side, Royal Victoria Dock, one of several busy junctions in the docks, in 1949.

Department. Exchange Sidings had 70 miles of track and could accommodate 1,500 wagons. Some shunting operations were also undertaken by horses and motor tractors. During the Second World War, the PLA steam locomotives – each with a crew of driver, fireman, head shunter and shunter – handled over 2,000 railway wagons each day.

This network employed an extensive rolling stock. In 1909 almost all the steam locomotives inherited from the dock companies were worn out. They were soon replaced. In 1915–16, for instance, 13 were delivered to the India and Millwall Docks alone. The last of the hundred or so steam locomotives owned by the Authority and its predecessors were delivered by Hudswell, Clarke & Co in 1953. By 1960, with the delivery of six diesel-electric engines, steam had disappeared from the dock railways. Rail traffic had declined from 41 per cent of total quayside traffic in 1938 to just 12 per cent. Even so, the PLA ran 27 diesel locomotives and 520 rail wagons over 140 miles of track until 1965 when it was decided that the competition from road haulage had become too great. By then, less than two per cent of the Port's traffic used the railways.

This was far from the end of rail haulage in the Port. Containers were ideal for carriage by rail and, as quayside rail operations in the old docks ended, a new rail terminal was opened at Tilbury in 1970. More than two decades later, after the eventual privatisation of Tilbury, a new multi-million pound rail terminal was opened. Congested motorways and rising environmental concerns continue to give rail freight a new lease of life in the Port, with a number of aggregates terminals rail linked and Lafarge re-establishing a rail link into its Thurrock terminal.

Several PLA locomotives gathered in the Royal Docks in October 1954. Diesels replaced steam in 1960.

The boat train at No.1 Berth, Tilbury, in 1958.

After 1945, under Lord Waverley and Leslie Ford, successive Chief Engineers, Wilfred Shepherd-Barron and, from 1953, George Wilson, supervised the rebuilding of the docks. The Authority was encouraged by the government's confidence, expressed before the end of the war by Herbert Morrison in particular, that London, along with other east-coast ports, was best placed to make the most from post-war reconstruction. It was not an easy task and almost exhausted the Authority's resources. With Britain almost bankrupt, it was crucial to bring the Port back into full operation and help the nation's export drive.

As cargo handling methods changed, the PLA concentrated its resources at Tilbury. No.34 Berth, shown here around 1970, was the first berth purpose-built to handle packaged timber, first seen in the UK in 1958.

Yet, apart from war damage reparations, there was no state aid to rebuild the UK's leading port. With British factories worn out by the war effort, orders for new machinery sometimes took years to fulfil. The last of the 112 electric cranes ordered by the PLA between 1948 and 1950 was delivered only in 1955. The Authority had to fall back on a lot of second-hand equipment, including 33 diesel mobile cranes. Although the PLA's plans suffered in particular from a shortage of steel, leading to many works being carried out in concrete, the PLA was helped by the influence of the Chairman, Lord Waverley, who secured some preferential allocation of scarce materials and equipment. This was in line with the government's view that the Port was ideally suited to the export of high-value heavy items, including locomotives and railway carriages, buses and motor cars. But the efforts of the PLA were not matched by those of the state, which, financially weakened by post-war economic difficulties, proved unable to fund the much-needed improved road links to the docks.

Reconstruction enabled many of the docks to benefit, at least in part, from large modern sheds, equipped with electric trucks, mobile cranes and fork-lift trucks. By the early 1960s, as well as 750 cranes of various types and sizes, the PLA was operating more than a hundred fork-lift trucks. This process of modernisation was extended under Leslie Ford and his successor, Dudley Perkins, as new methods of handling cargo were introduced, from roll-on roll-off vessels to containers. By the late 1960s, the obvious consequence of these trends was declining trade for the up-river docks.

The Surrey Commercial Docks enjoyed an Indian summer. In the early post-war years as many as 600 barges would crowd the docks but the clearance of bombed warehouses also provided space to expand the road network and improve distribution by road haulage. The PLA invested heavily in mechanisation. Fork-lift trucks had made their first appearance in the docks at the East India Dock in the late 1940s, introduced by the stevedoring firm, Scruttons. Soon afterwards, enthusiastically supported by younger, forward-looking PLA managers, they were adopted in the Surrey Commercial Docks. In conjunction with the use of mobile cranes and new purpose-built sheds, they allowed stacks of timber, piled on pallets, to be doubled in height. The capacity of a typical shed rose from two thousand to seven thousand tons. Output was transformed. One man handled just a few pieces of loose timber at a time; a fork-lift truck could carry five tons at once.

The Royal Docks were still the jewel in the PLA's crown. Alongside reconstruction work, new methods of working were introduced. With the arrival of fork-lift trucks at the Royal Albert Docks, it was possible to replace seven trucking gangs of eight men each with two gangs of three men each. A shed gang working export cargo, using mobile cranes and fork-lift trucks, could handle 300 tons a day, compared with only 50 tons using hand trucks.

In 1956 the old ambitious plans for a new north dock were dusted off and the Royal Group of Docks Extension Scheme was approved. This was never implemented even though the PLA believed at one time that the Royals were well-suited for the new cargo-handling methods. The Authority began experimenting with containers at the Royal Victoria Dock. No. 4 Berth and Quay were completed there in 1960 to serve a continental container service. The transit shed, 700 by 200 feet (213 metres by 61 metres), without any internal columns and with ample clearance for mobile cranes, was the largest in the docks. In the mid-1960s the Royals still handled by far the largest proportion of all goods discharged in the enclosed docks, double the volume of the next busiest, the India and Millwall Docks.

After the war the India and Millwall Docks were an amalgam of the old and, where possible, the new. At the West India Docks work began in 1951 on the PLA's first mechanised export berth, intended as a prototype for similar improvements elsewhere. At the devastated Rum Quay new berths were built for handling fruit. On the other hand, despite the destruction of seven of the nine tall Georgian sugar warehouses, the old North Quay remained much as it had before the war, with cobbled roads, narrow quays and two-storey quayside warehouses dating from the First World War. Here there was little mechanisation and traditional methods of working, including the use of hand trucks, continued.

Millwall Docks were transformed between 1957 and 1967, with huge new transit sheds, electric platform trucks and fork-lifts, modern cranes and loading banks to remove the double handling of goods from lorries. Those who led the PLA appreciated the productivity gains yielded by mechanisation, as did the stevedoring companies and shipping lines. One obstacle to doing even more was resistance from the dockworkers. Dudley Perkins, the PLA's Director-General, admitted in 1965 that more could

have been done, 'were it not for the fear of redundancy that is still very real among the dockers'. As a result, the PLA was often forced to negotiate agreements on mechanisation berth by berth.

At this time the Authority was still convinced that the newer methods of carrying cargo would catch on only gradually and that ships would have to carry conventional cargoes for the foreseeable future. As a result, the PLA continued investing in conventional cargo-handling facilities both at Millwall and the Royal Docks until the end

The Royal Albert Dock pictured in 1951.
The floating crane is the *London Titan*. The Royal Docks remained the jewel in the PLA's crown after 1945.

of the 1960s. At Millwall, this investment included a new terminal designed by Norman Foster for the Fred Olsen Line, opened in 1969.

At the smallest docks, the London and St Katharine, new shed and quayside cranes were added after the war, and the number of berths was increased to 29, almost all of them at the London Dock. But any further development was halted in 1965. The warehousing that had once made these and other up-river docks so important was no longer essential. The progressive growth of imports for immediate distribution made investment in specialised facilities for quick handling and delivery more important.

Tilbury had been one of the least busy of the enclosed docks before 1939. After 1945 Tilbury quickly took third place behind the Royals and the India and Millwall Docks. In 1946 the first ro-ro services in the UK began at Tilbury, when three converted tank-landing ships ran a service for the British forces to Hamburg. This was replaced by a service to Antwerp in 1957 and to Rotterdam in 1960. Tilbury benefited from the modernisation work carried out during the 1950s and early 1960s. A new grain terminal was built, ten deep-water berths were added for general cargo, with modern sheds equipped with fork-lift trucks, and the passenger terminal was modernised.

The last vaultmen and coopers pose to record the last barrel out of London Docks in 1969.

The latter investment was based upon the continuing passenger traffic passing through Tilbury. In the first years after the war ships left Tilbury with British emigrants for Australia. In 1948 the *Empire Windrush* docked at Tilbury, bringing the first large post-war group of West Indian immigrants to the country. It was still possible for passengers to sail from Tilbury for destinations varying from Gothenburg with Swedish Lloyd, to India, the Far East and Australia with what became P&O-Orient Lines. The Port as a whole was bustling with passenger ships calling on all parts of the world well into the 1960s. The Aznar Line sailed from the Pool of London for Spain and

Madeira, the MacAndrews' fleet headed for the Mediterranean from the London Dock, and the Prince Line left South West India Dock for the Eastern Mediterranean and North Africa. From the Royal Docks P&O's liners still ran to the Far East and Shaw Savill vessels to the Antipodes.

From the early 1960s investment in Tilbury was increased. The PLA, anticipating the importance of containerisation and unitised cargo, was convinced of the need for an ocean container port in the south-east. The pre-war position, when goods were shipped into London and then transhipped to the Continent, no longer applied.

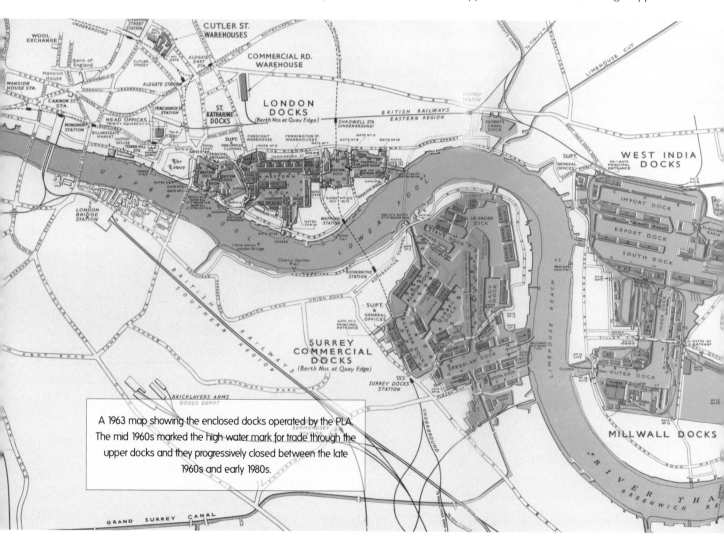

A 1963 map showing the enclosed docks operated by the PLA. The mid 1960s marked the high water mark for trade through the upper docks and they progressively closed between the late 1960s and early 1980s.

...inental ports,
...t, without the
...ndon, and then
...ch as Felixstowe
...the way Britain's
...ng, with the main
...vealth towards the
...for Tilbury were
...he Port. At the time
...g UK port authorities
...r berths. On the other
...such improvements,

which provoked much criticism from the leaders of UK ports, including the Port of London.

At Tilbury, the first stage of the PLA's investment plans produced two new deep-water export berths and two berths for the new generation of ro-ro short sea ferries. In 1965, following his conversion to containerisation, Dudley Perkins was writing that Tilbury 'may well become the focal point of the port'. Within the next few years Tilbury became the Port's principal terminal for timber, grain and the container trade. Following the widespread adoption of packaged timber in the early 1960s, a specialist timber handling berth, No. 34, was

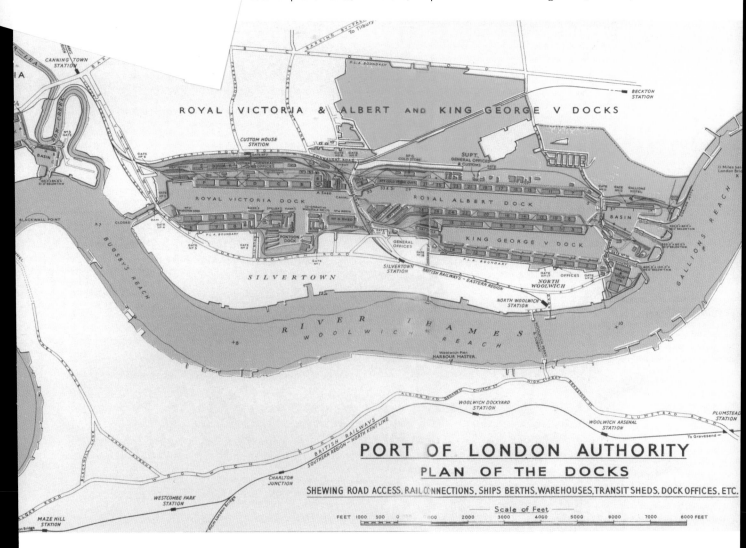

PORT OF LONDON AUTHORITY
PLAN OF THE DOCKS
SHEWING ROAD ACCESS, RAIL CONNECTIONS, SHIPS BERTHS, WAREHOUSES, TRANSIT SHEDS, DOCK OFFICES, ETC.

Scale of Feet

FEET 1000 500 0 1000 2000 3000 4000 5000 6000 7000 8000 FEET opened in 1966. By then, seven berths for handling unitised cargo had been completed. New berths were leased to tenants as a plain quay and apron, with an area of land behind, the tenant providing the buildings and equipment. In 1967 a further dedicated timber berth, developed with Svenska Cellulosa, was opened.

'The commercial response to this enterprise,' recorded The PLA Monthly, 'has exceeded expectations.' This was hardly surprising given the huge improvement in efficiency. The PLA successfully negotiated changes to the ganging system, creating flexible and interchangeable weekly-paid 20-strong shed crews. More than 4,000 tons of timber could be discharged in a ten-hour working day at these specialist berths. Two decades later the Spring Vega would discharge a record of more than 30,000 tonnes of timber.

In 1969 a new bulk grain terminal was opened. This made it possible to sell the obsolete floating grain elevators in the Royal Docks. In the same year plans for a major new container berth were disrupted by industrial action taken by the dockworkers. This delayed by 18 months the opening of a purpose-built berth for the new Australian container service to be operated by Overseas Containers Ltd (OCL) and Associated Container Transport (ACT). The annual report of the PLA in 1969 observed that 'the damage this has done ... to the reputation of the Port is incalculable'. This was a critical period for the Port, with Felixstowe's Landguard container terminal already in operation, and the PLA's leadership distracted by ambitious plans for Maplin.

Just as Tilbury's new container berths were coming into use, the PLA, with several other partners, including Shell and the construction firm Mowlem, formed the Thames Estuary Development Company to explore the development of Maplin Sands, off Foulness Island. This location would have overcome a perceived disadvantage of Tilbury, being 35 miles from the mouth of the estuary (but at the same time, 35 miles closer to the market). It was hoped that a combined deep-sea oil terminal and deep-sea and short-sea container port, with integrated

road and rail links, would be in operation at Maplin from 1976–77. The proposal became hopelessly entangled with the issue of a third London airport and never reached fruition. Almost four decades later, government approval was given to create a similarly ambitious port complex, London Gateway, at Shell Haven.

Despite this sideshow and other disruptions, the Port's container trade made rapid progress and in the early 1970s Tilbury was the UK's leading container port. Once again, the improvement in productivity was dramatic. One container berth could handle the equivalent of ten conventional cargo berths. A container ship could be turned round in 36 hours, rather than the ten to 14 days required for a conventional cargo ship.

The cost of constructing new container berths was a major capital investment for the PLA. Each one took two years to build and another two years before generating an adequate return. At the same time the Authority was losing money from a decline in conventional cargo, a continued lack of progress in modernising working practices and the impact of the decasualisation of dock labour. The speed with which containerisation was adopted after 1965 caught the Authority by surprise. The combined impact of all this could be met only by rationalising conventional cargo-handling operations and ultimately closing docks. The first to close was the East India Import Dock in 1967, followed by London and St Katharine in 1968. At Trinity Square, one member of staff clearly saw where this was leading, and fixed 'Docks Closed' notices on the huge and impressive model of the docks in the foyer. At the now loss-making Surrey Docks, Lady Dock was filled in and Lavender Dock partly filled in during 1968, as the volume of timber discharged continued to fall. Limited to vessels of around 10,000 tons, the configuration of the docks could not cope with the advent of packaged timber in much larger ships. The docks closed following the departure of the last timber ship, the Russian Kandalakshales, on 22 December 1970.

Every year more and more general berths were closed in the remaining docks. Shipping moved progres-

Two years after closure, the Royal Docks were no longer a hub for trade, but home to laid up Greek-owned ships. (Museum of London)

sively down river. In 1976, for instance, Fred Olsen Lines moved to Tilbury, giving up the Millwall terminal it had taken over only seven years before. The future of the docks became a matter of greater political concern and the government pressured the PLA into agreeing to keep the remaining upper docks open. This was in spite of the fact that there was no longer sufficient business for them. Their operating costs, hindered by out-of-date working practices, were crippling. Even at Tilbury, overmanning placed the docks at a disadvantage compared with its non-Dock Labour Scheme rivals, particularly Felixstowe. In the upper docks further investment was out of the question; as Sir John Cuckney, the PLA's Chairman, put it in 1978, 'in all honesty, there is no commercial justification for it'.

At the same time the PLA was also bearing the cost of surplus labour as employer of last resort. In 1975, when an unofficial strike in the Royal Docks brought about the collapse of Scruttons, the stevedoring firm, the PLA was compelled to take over their business just to guarantee there were enough stevedores for the shipping still using the docks. In 1978, when the upper docks lost £9 million (£37 million in today's prices), the PLA's registered workforce rose by more than 500 as workers from failed firms were taken on.

For a time the Royal Docks benefited from business displaced from the docks that had already closed but operations were gradually wound down throughout the 1970s. By 1979 there were just ten operational berths left in the Royal Docks. In the following summer, the India and Millwall Docks were closed, with the exception of the Montague Meyer timber berth and the bulk wine installation. Cargo handling was transferred to the Royal Docks and Tilbury. On 26 October 1981, with the discharge of the Chinese vessel *Xingfeng*, the Royal Docks finally closed to shipping. The scrap-metal business continued until 1983 when it was transferred to Tilbury. In the same year the Meyer business was relocated from Millwall to Tilbury. For another two years the Royal Docks were used for laid-up shipping. The last shipping movements

through the Royals were in November 1985. The docks, once so busy, once so proud, were a sad sight, with redundant ships laid up, grass growing through the crane tracks along the quays, rail lines ripped up and buildings falling into disrepair.

The closure of the docks made land available for redevelopment. For a variety of reasons, the PLA never fully capitalised upon this opportunity. As a public-service organisation, not an entrepreneurial business, it lacked expertise in commercial property. It was accused of selling off property too cheaply. St Katharine Dock, sold to the GLC in 1968, and East India Dock, sold to the Central Electricity Generating Board in 1971, each fetched just £1.5 million (£17 million in today's prices). The sale of St Katharine Dock was particularly contentious as the GLC quickly sold it on to Taylor Woodrow for a premium of several million pounds. The PLA's head office in Trinity Square was also sold in 1971 for a profit of just £7 million (around £70 million today). Further sales were delayed by the Docklands Study, commissioned by the government in 1971. By the time it reported two years later, the property boom of the early 1970s was over. The market had passed its peak by the time a joint-venture company, Riverside London, was formed in 1973 for the redevelopment of London Docks. There was, in any case, no real appreciation of how valuable the PLA estate might be for redevelopment. The proposals made by Riverside London envisaged not commercial development but a new head office for the PLA, a new site for the City Polytechnic, new PLA warehousing and 2,000 local-authority houses.

With property prices depressed for the rest of the 1970s, the land was valued as derelict. It was either developed piecemeal by the PLA or sold off to local authorities, particularly the GLC and the three main dockland boroughs of Southwark, Tower Hamlets and Newham. The Docklands Joint Committee, representing these local authorities, plus Greenwich and Lewisham, advocated ambitious proposals but lacked influence and resources. Land at the London Dock and the Surrey Commercial Docks was sold during 1976–77 to Tower Hamlets,

A warehouse and quayside at the Royal Docks in 1987 – the bustle of the 1960s long gone as ships became larger and containerisation took hold. (Museum of London)

MECHANISATION AND CONTAINERS

The post-war revolution in cargo handling began with pallets and the fork-lift truck. When they were introduced around 1951 to the reconstructed 'H' shed on the north side of the South Dock at West India Docks, their impact was immediate. The men willingly moved from a gang system to a shed crew system, working for a guaranteed wage rather than piece-work rates. With a minimum of ten men, supplemented by others when necessary, the operation was run with an average of 24 men, rather than 72 under the traditional system.

Nearly 20 years later, the revolution was completed by the advent of the standardised container. In 1968 Tilbury received the first-ever transatlantic container ship, the *American Lancer*. Arriving at 5.15 pm on 2 June, she discharged her cargo and reloaded before sailing 13 hours later. Her cargo was made up entirely of standardised containers, whose dimensions had been agreed internationally in 1965.

The contrast in productivity compared with traditional methods was immense – the discharge of a conventional cargo vessel carrying 11,000 tons required 72 men on board, 18 on the quay and 12 in the shed; whereas a container vessel with up to 400 ten-ton containers on board needed only two men on the cranes, two on the ship, five or six driving the straddle carriers, two on the quay and a general yard man. From no containers at all in 1966, over 800,000 TEU (twenty foot equivalent units) of containers are handled at Tilbury today.

The way forward - a painting from 1958 by Lawrence Wright of No.4 Berth at the Royal Victoria Dock, with a modern shed suitable for use with pallets and fork-lift trucks.

Early trials of container cargoes at No.4 Berth, Royal Victoria Dock, in 1964.

WESTBOURNE

Southwark and the GLC, and developed mainly for mixed housing. In an area that had suffered economically, the PLA developed industrial start-up units to encourage employment, and also to bring in rental income. Piecemeal disposals continued. In 1978 the old East India Company warehouses at Cutler Street were sold for £5 million (£21 million in today's prices) and developed into offices. In 1979 Riverside London sold its interest in land at London Docks to News International for its controversial new Wapping printing works. In 1982 Billingsgate Fish Market was persuaded to relocate from Lower Thames Street to the site of 36 Shed, North Quay at West India Dock, bringing 700 jobs from the City. Small business units and housing were developed at West India and Millwall Docks. Land in the Royal Docks was leased for the construction of what became the City Airport in 1987.

Little of the proceeds from any of the sales made by the PLA after 1968 were used for reinvestment in the Port. Instead, with successive governments unwilling to reform the National Dock Labour Scheme, the money kept surplus dockers in employment and then helped to pay them off.

It was Margaret Thatcher's Conservative government which first appreciated the potential of the vast areas of disused land in the docks for urban redevelopment and regeneration. To realise this, the London Docklands Development Corporation (LDDC) was formed in 1981 and an Enterprise Zone was created on the Isle of Dogs in 1982. It was the significant investment made by LDDC in the modern, permanent infrastructure on the sites of the old docks that made them financially attractive to commercial developers for the first time. The LDDC progressively took over key sites from the PLA, starting with an initial vesting order covering land including Canary Wharf in 1981.

The PLA retained operational land, but this was progressively transferred to LDDC as it fell out of use. The relationship between the two organisations was generally good but sometimes tense. In 1983, when the Royal Victoria Dock was sold, the PLA was served with a

The closure of the enclosed docks was the catalyst for the transformation of Docklands. Here the redeveloped Canary Wharf forms the backdrop to the PLA's launch, *Westbourne*, on the river in 2008.

compulsory purchase order for other land in the Royal Docks when discussions over alternative approaches to land ownership were still under way between the two sides. In 1985 the PLA agreed a long lease with the LDDC on 125 acres of land at Royal Docks, with options for the sale of the freehold over the following five years. The building at the same time of the Docklands Light Railway accelerated the transfer of PLA land for commercial use.

For the development of land not transferred to the LDDC, the PLA formed a subsidiary company, Port of London Properties (POLP), in 1984. Over the next few years a series of profitable joint developments took place, including an ASDA superstore on the Isle of Dogs, the Wood Wharf Business Park, Poplar Business Park, Waterside and Clippers Quay at Millwall Dock, Park Gate at Beckton and Jamestown Harbour close to Canary Wharf.

Again little of the money received either from the LDDC or from developments carried out by POLP could be reinvested in the Port. Instead, these funds were allocated for the repayment of the severance grants given by the government. Eventually the government agreed with the PLA in 1994 that it would write off the outstanding liability owed by the PLA in return for the proceeds from the orderly sale of remaining property. In 2001 the Authority was also asked to sell to British Waterways the valuable 20-acre site at Wood Wharf, next to Canary Wharf. On completion of this sale, POLP's active involvement in development drew to a close.

While it was gradually closing the other docks, the PLA continued to invest in Tilbury. As well as a new rail terminal in 1970, a new West African terminal was opened in 1973. In 1978 the Northfleet Hope container terminal was opened for OCL and ACT, featuring the biggest refrigerated container storage facility of any port in the world at the time.

In 1985 Tilbury's cruise terminal was modernised and renamed the London International Cruise Terminal. The growth of the international airlines had led to the slow decline of passenger liners but over time this trend was reversed, accelerating in recent years. At the same time, as

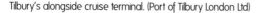
Tilbury's alongside cruise terminal. (Port of Tilbury London Ltd)

part of the Authority's policy of encouraging alternative uses of the upper and middle reaches of the river, Central London Cruise Moorings actively marketed upstream moorings for smaller cruise ships close by Tower Bridge and at Greenwich. Today London has established an important niche in the cruise market, served both by Tilbury's alongside terminal and the mid-stream moorings further up river.

By now, Tilbury had become a complete port complex in its own right. Among Tilbury's tenants were major millers, with their own processing facilities, and several timber importers, as well as OCL and ACT. The docks were also given a boost through the improvement of road links on the completion of the M25 in 1986.

By the late 1980s, more than six million tonnes of cargo was passing through Tilbury every year. Yet the

docks, as a separate division of the PLA, were still unprofitable because they were badly overmanned. After 1989, freed at last from the shackles of the National Dock Labour Scheme, and preparing for privatisation, Tilbury achieved profitability once more. Better productivity produced a 40 per cent increase in the number of containers handled. Within a year of the abolition of the scheme, Tilbury had won 19 new services. The port was privatised on 11 March 1992, sold for £32 million (£52 million in today's prices) to the existing management, with the overwhelming support of employees. Three years later, the Port of Tilbury, the UK's leading forest products port, second-largest cruise-passenger port and third-largest container port, became part of Forth Ports for £132 million (£183 million in today's prices).

Centred around its dock complex, the Port of Tilbury is a thriving logistics hub, handling over ten million tonnes of cargo a year.
(Port of Tilbury London Ltd.)

The PLA licenses almost 600 vessels used on the river. To meet the demanding schedule of inspections the PLA employs two full-time, professional marine surveyors, and is the only port authority to do so.

Photo shows PLA Deputy Harbour Master (SMS), Mark Towens and Marine Surveyor, Tim Prior.

WORKING FOR THE PLA

The PLA at its peak was a huge organisation. For many years it was the single largest employer in the Port. Its structure was complex and covered a wide variety of occupations. Most of its staff were employed in the docks, ranging from dockers on the quayside and in the sheds to an army of clerks in the dock offices and the police on the dock gates. For many years almost all of them were men. The whole operation was overseen from the PLA's impressive headquarters in Trinity Square. For many staff, the PLA was not just the focus of their working lives, it was also the focus of their social lives, offering an array of sporting and social activities. The work of the PLA, and the way in which it looked after its workforce, bred a spirit of pride and loyalty among its employees. Today, with many fewer staff, of whom the pilots form the largest group, that spirit still exists.

For most of its history the PLA employed more people in the Port of London than any other single employer. In 1910 the workforce numbered 11,297. Ninety per cent of them were dockworkers – 5,074 'perms', 2,123 other regularly employed men and an average of 2,944 extra men taken on daily. The remaining ten per cent (1,156) covered staff working at head office and in the dock offices as well as the Authority's marine personnel. Numbers seem to have peaked in 1911, when they reached 13,249, but they remained around this figure for the next 50 years. In the early 1960s the PLA still employed 12,000 people. Thereafter numbers gradually shrank, reflecting changes in the industry, declining to 8,925 in 1973 and 6,670 in 1980. By then, as employer of last resort, the PLA accounted for two-thirds of the total registered dock labour force in the Port. In 1991, when the PLA's workforce numbered 1,408, more than half of them were still dock workers. The last of the dockers left the PLA with the privatisation of Tilbury in 1992. The Authority was left with 464 staff, of whom marine pilots formed the largest group. Today the PLA employs 360 staff working across a range of activities including navigational safety, marine services and administration.

The picture says it all – hardworking, resilient and cheerful – a London docker in 1950.

As a public authority, the PLA was for decades a highly structured and hierarchical organisation. The Authority inherited many working practices and traditions from the old dock companies, as well as the Thames Conservancy, integrating their staff into the new organisation.

The complexity of it all becomes clear after glancing through the *PLA Staff Supplements,* published every month from January 1927 until the end of 1954. The diverse range of positions varied from a First Class Foreman in the Southern & Bulk Grain Department, Royal Victoria Dock, and a Second Class Clerk, Wood & Tonnage Dues Office, Surrey Commercial Docks, to a First Class Writer, North Eastern Department, Royal Albert Dock, and a First Class Calculator Operator, Finance Accounts Section, Accounting Department. This was just the administrative staff of the Port Authority – the list of occupations in the docks and on the river was equally long and varied.

The example of one man, Henry Norris, illustrates the way in which an employee could make his way through this hierarchy. Norris was 58 years old when he was transferred to the PLA in 1909. Aged 16, he had joined the East and West India Dock Company as a Writer in the General Office at the West India Dock. He was promoted to Third Class and then Second Class Clerk and moved on to become an Assistant Warehousekeeper, Warehousekeeper and First Class Warehousekeeper. He was then appointed as an Assistant Superintendent and in 1909 he held the rank of Superintendent. In 1911 he became Chief Superintendent of Docks and Warehouses, from which post he retired in 1920.

Norris's progression was not typical of the careers followed by most members of the PLA's staff. With an army of clerks required to administer the work of the docks, opportunities for promotion were often limited. In 1909 the new Authority was filled with men in their 50s who sometimes rose no further than Third Class Clerk. Half a century later the position was much the same. As a new junior clerical officer in 1955, Geoff Ennals found that the path to becoming what was then a Grade 1 Clerical Officer largely depended on waiting for someone either to retire or die.

The work of the PLA's marine staff is often taken for granted yet without it activity on the river would grind to a halt. Here crewmen on board a screwing lighter prepare to lay a screw for a mooring buoy on the river in 1948.

A small boy takes a peep at a dock constable on gate duty at Greenland Gate in the Surrey Commercial Docks in 1955.

PLA clerks at work in a dock shed office in 1925.

One reason for this was that many employees, dockers as much as salaried staff, spent their entire working lives with the PLA. In 1927, for instance, T A Harrison, a Second Class Clerk, retired after 52 years and W S Ellis, a Third Class Clerk, after 49 years; while in 1930 T J Lockhart, a First Class Clerk, retired after 48 years, having spent the last 39 years of his career at the India and Millwall Control. This was not unusual among large organisations during the first half of the twentieth century but, unlike some others, this tradition has been sustained at the PLA throughout its history. Geoff Ennals, for instance, who rose to become Secretary, retired in 2002 after 47 years, while there are several members of the current staff, such as Ian Flanders and Martin Round, who have been with the Authority for more than 40 years.

Another reason why it was sometimes difficult for employees to find opportunities for promotion was that the Authority tended to recruit staff in waves. This happened, for instance, at the end of each world war.

As staff began to retire, from the mid-1930s and again from the mid-1950s, and promotions opened up vacancies for juniors, the Authority filled the gaps by appointing able young school leavers from local secondary schools. Among them in the 1930s were Dick Butler, who joined in 1936, and Cyril Webb, who joined in 1937. Serving a two-year apprenticeship, they worked in various departments, attended monthly lectures and studied commerce, benefiting greatly from the tuition generously given by their long-serving colleagues.

There were other obstacles to promotion. In the docks junior clerks only made progress once they had learnt to swim. This was a requirement for all dock staff, stemming apparently from the loss through drowning one foggy night in 1873 of 17 men employed by the East and West India Docks Company. At Head Office, junior clerks were expected to attain dictation at a hundred words a minute and competence at transcribing shorthand before they were considered for advancement.

RITES OF PASSAGE

For those beginning their working lives, the docks and Head Office could seem daunting places. At the offices, boys and young men were introduced to a world where routine, hierarchies, formality and supervision were the rule. For many, a sense of schoolroom discipline continued. The uniformed boy messengers, for instance, were inspected every day, and members of the public would often report them for misdemeanours, such as cap throwing and loitering by shop windows. It was a world where – before the First World War, at least – formally dressed clerks shook hands with each other at the beginning and end of work.

There could, however, also be a sense of fun. Whilst more senior staff were always addressed as 'Mister', many – especially the grumpy 'jobsworths' – were given irreverent nicknames. Young office workers – whenever out of sight of their supervisors – also engaged in well-honed banter. For those starting manual careers, there were also more 'humorous' rites of passage. Boys at the various dock workshops might be sent to the stores for left-handed hammers, right-handed spanners and rainbow paint. Even the less innocent fell for the trick of being sent to ask for 'a long weight' – with the inevitable, boring, result. Sometimes the jokes were not appreciated. One example was sending new boys to assist at the stores. On arrival, they would be told that they would 'be doing the diving' the next day, and then be dressed – with full ceremony - in large and heavy diving suits. The joke was often only discovered after work, when concerned parents questioned their obviously anxious sons. Others fell for the old latrine trick, whereby some wag would float a flaming paper boat down the open drain beneath the line of toilet seats. These more humorous rites of passage reflected a subversive and rebellious response to the world of rules and regulations.

Youngsters began work for the PLA as boy messengers at the age of 14, in their smart uniforms, with caps and letter pouches. This young man is on an errand in the Royal Albert Dock in 1935.

Although career development was inconsistent, the sheer size of the PLA did allow those with ambition and determination to find a way to rise through the organisation. Both Henry Norris and Geoff Ennals, their careers separated by half a century, achieved this, as did Dick

Canadian flour, rather than the snow, is responsible for the dusting given to these dockers, loading a cargo set onto an electric truck during the Second World War.

Butler, who eventually became Director of Docks, and Cyril Webb, ultimately appointed as the PLA's representative in Australia. By the 1960s, with greater emphasis on training, and the introduction of a separate examination to accelerate the ascent of talented juniors, a more structured approach to career development opened up greater opportunities for PLA staff.

For many years entrants to the PLA were divided between Major and Minor Staff, or, as they later became, the Upper Division and Lower Division, the former being the equivalent of the civil service fast stream. Major Staff were recruited by examination at 16, either taking charge of Minor Staff clerks or assistant foremen, or employed in office work. Those who chose to move outside the office could work their way up from Warehousekeeper to Superintendent, while those who remained in the office could aim for the heights as Principal or Chief Clerk. Occasionally promotion offered an alternative way for PLA employees to join the Major Staff. Charles Connor, for instance, who joined the PLA in 1912 as an apprentice cooper, reached the Major Staff through his salaried appointment as Foreman Cooper and Vaultkeeper.

A boy joined the Minor Staff when he entered the docks at 14. Until he was 17 he served as a Boy Messenger, running around the City and the docks all day. Success in his examination entitled him to become a foreman's assistant, with the chance to move on from Third Class to First Class Foreman. If he failed, he became a labouring boy until 21, when he could join the ranks of the 'perms'. With dockers often earning more money than foremen, some boys were known to fail their exams deliberately.

Clerks joining the Authority at any time between 1909 until the late 1950s could expect to find themselves based in the dock offices, sitting on high stools at sloping desks in front of massive ledgers, often repeating the same tasks day in, day out. In 1912, 16-year-old R B Oram joined the PLA as a Fourth Class Clerk in the General Office at London Docks. Sixty clerks sat in one room, overseen by the Principal Clerk from his raised glass box.

The tally clerk was an indispensable member of the PLA's quayside team.
Here a tally clerk checks goods in a transit shed before the Second World War.

In the basement kitchen a cook provided food and drink – hot coffee and dripping toast for a penny were much appreciated in wintertime. Beyond the kitchen lay six earth closets for staff, in full view of the dining tables – to use them, staff applied for the key to their senior clerk, who carefully noted in his ledger the time of issue and return. In the early 1960s, several years after Oram's retirement, newly appointed Bob Aspinall found that the dock office at Surrey Commercial Docks had changed hardly at all, still filled with clerks at their high stools and sloping desks.

There were few women in Oram's early days. Typically outnumbered ten to one in the office by men, and working largely in 'unseen' positions, such as typists, telephonists and comptometer operators. When Elizabeth Garrett joined the typing room at Tilbury before the Second World War, young girls were expected to wear navy blue overalls to avoid distracting the men. In the mid-1950s the only two women in the Dock Office at Surrey Commercial Docks were comptometer operators. Other than Head Office or the Dock Offices, women were found only in the warehouses. More women had been recruited by the mid-1960s, much to the disgruntlement of one docks superintendent, who blamed women in the office for feeding the cats and making them lose interest in catching rats.

This conservatism was not unusual within the PLA. In R B Oram's experience, managers were often unimaginative and petty-minded, clinging to outdated practices, whether it was how things were done on the quayside or the way discipline was administered in the office. On the quayside Geoff Ennals discovered that 'the operational side of the PLA … is a very macho sort of place. There's a lot of posturing. They all think they're hard men, strict disciplinarians, and come up the hard way, and you've got to serve the same apprenticeship they did. They didn't see why it should be made any easier for you.' For Oram and those managers who returned to the PLA after 1945, this approach was deeply frustrating. It appears to have eased only from the late 1950s, as the next generation, men like Dick Butler, Stan Turner and John Gabony, achieved promotion.

HEAD OFFICE

Head Office, known as 'Trap One' or the 'Town House', was a world apart, with its wood-panelled boardrooms and committee rooms, lifts and toilets reserved for Board members, and different canteens for different grades of staff. Here too were the library and archive, an invaluable resource, opened to staff from 1926 onwards for research and information.

For many Head Office staff, the docks were a foreign country they had no intention of visiting. According to R B Oram, in 45 years with the PLA, he 'could count on the fingers of one hand the occasions when top management ever visited the docks'. On the other hand, the office of the Chief Engineer from 1909 until 1985 was located on the Royal Albert Dock.

When the Trinity Square building opened in 1922, it was linked directly to the docks by an extensive new telephone network, operated by female telephonists from a large exchange. Elizabeth Garrett, who transferred to Trinity Square after 20 years at Tilbury, found even in the 1950s that it was very prim, proper and po-faced.

These were the days when a firm, Collars Ltd, would come round the offices to take away dirty stiff collars and bring clean ones, when suits were worn Monday to Fridays, but when only a blazer and slacks would do on the half a dozen Saturdays staff were expected to work every year.

When Keith Doggett moved to Trinity Square in 1964, he discovered that Head Office staff even had different working hours, with the privilege of starting at 9.15 am, a quarter of an hour later than dock staff.

The petty distinctions between grades were epitomised by the entitlement at a middling grade to one's own battered aluminium tea tray and tea set for the afternoon tea break.

Mischief-makers among the younger staff would mix up the bowler hats left on the table by the senior clerks when they took their liquid lunch each Friday. 'Naughty boys' picked out by the Authority were destined to spend their days in the dead-end of the Port Rates department, from which there was no escape other than to leave the Authority.

Women typists working under strict supervision in the book-keeping room at Head Office in 1930. They were an invaluable part of the organisation.

Top: Clerks at work in the reconstructed rotunda at Trinity Square around 1950.

Bottom: The smoking room at the PLA Luncheon Club in St Katharine Dock House around 1935.

Dockers waiting for the call-on at the Royal Docks in 1962. This practice disappeared only in 1967 when the future of dock labour was already under threat.

Among the dockers, who for eight decades made up most of the PLA's workforce, the hierarchy was less complicated: there were 'perms', 'prefs' and casuals. The PLA employed all three, unlike the many hundreds of other Port employers. Most employed only a handful of 'perms', if any at all, taking on casual labour on a daily basis. With regular employment, the 'perms' were the aristocrats among the dockers. Proud of this reputation, the PLA 'perms' were often reluctant to jeopardise their position by going out on strike. When the wife of one wag among the casual labourers complained her hairstyle was coming out, he told her to ask her hairdresser for a 'PLA perm' since 'they never come out'.

Regular work was a precious commodity among dockers before the Second World War. The fear of unemployment and the degrading spectacle of the call-on had turned possession of a place on the register, introduced in 1921, and, even more, a prized place among the PLA's 'perms', into privileges that many fathers passed on to their sons, reinforcing the legendary solidarity of the dockers from generation to generation. The call-on endured by the casual dockers was a degrading experi-

The hooks and hand-trucks were for generations the stock-in-trade of the docker, disappearing only with the advent of containers.

ence. Bill Wardell, a 'nonner', or non-registered man, described how it operated in the 1930s, when work was scarce:

'At quarter to eight in the morning the foreman came out and stood in the road, eyeing the men up and down.

The registered men stood with their cards in their hands. They were called first. After that everything became a shambles. All the nonners was pushing and shoving, and calling the foreman. Then he threw the tickets into the air and watched the men scramble and fight for them. I came out with the arm of my sleeve all ripped but I got half a day's work.'

There were 400 coopers in the docks in the late nineteenth century but just 45 were left in 1966. Apprentices could rise to become foremen coopers or ultimately vaultkeepers. The wine cooper was a skilled craftsmen but after wine began to be delivered in bulk most of them had to spend much of their time knocking up boxes. The last two coopers employed by the PLA were Len Preston and John Ardley, who were made redundant in December 1982.

Another man, Bill Backhouse, remembered how things were so desperate in the depression that 'nonners' would rush a foreman and grab all the cards from his pocket. The men always stood back on the pavement, 'on the stones' as it was called, waiting to be called-on by the foreman in the middle of the road.

This humiliating ritual was mitigated, rather than abolished, with the introduction of the National Dock Labour Board in 1947, when the call-on was moved under cover. In return for their guaranteed weekly wage, men were expected to attend the so-called 'bomping box' twice a day, after the morning and lunchtime call-ons, in case labour was still needed. The last shreds of the call-on finally disappeared in 1972, with the abolition of the Temporarily Unattached Register.

Dock work was tough, physical labour in often

PORT TRADES

To the uninformed, all port work was undertaken by casual and unskilled 'dockers'. In reality, not only were dockers skilled, but port work formed a highly complex employment sector. Although most men worked at cargo handling – with ship discharge mostly undertaken by dockers, ship loading by stevedores, and quay and warehouse work by dockers, with lightermen manning the barges – there were many essential supporting trades.

In 1951, Paul Dehn's soundtrack for the PLA film, *Waters of Time*, listed some of the occupations at the Royal Docks:

'Dockers, tallymen, checkers, stevedores, hatchwaymen, winchmen, samplers, grain porters, timber porters, teamers, tacklemen, yardmasters, shunters, pilots, tug-boatmen, foyboatmen [watermen], fresh-watermen, blacksmiths, boilersmiths, masons, bricklayers, joiners, shipwrights, patternmakers, ship-chandlers, gangers, tractormen, coopers, bankriders, weighers, dock watchmen, dredgermen, launchmen, needlemen, jetty clerks, warehousemen, coal trimmers, lumpers and...policemen'.

A sugar sampler at work. The docks and warehouses boasted men with a wide variety of skills, testing the quality of a huge range of goods from all over the world.

The cooper was one of the many skilled craftsmen employed in the docks. The coopers formed their own society within the PLA.

Dehn, however, omitted some important groups who worked at both the Royals and the other docks. These included dockmasters, lockmen, berthing masters, cargo superintendents, traffic officers, divers, salvage crews, engineers, electricians, plumbers, painters, storemen, office staff, women canteen workers and Customs and Excise Officers. Many of these trades were also to be found along the wharves and river.

In addition, thousands of men and women found work in riverside power plants, processing works and factories. Port work – much of which was casual, based on teamwork and potentially dangerous – generated strong working and community bonds. Boys often followed their fathers' employment. After the war, employment peaked in 1955, with 31,448 registered dock workers – comprising 25,490 dockers and stevedores, 1,759 tally clerks and 4,199 lightermen. Changes in cargo handling methods, decasualisation, and the subsequent closure of the up-river docks and wharves, however, saw the number of registered dock workers reduced to 9,825 in 1975, and only 1,759 in 1988. By that time, most traditional port skills – built up over generations – had disappeared.

A vivid portrait of a meat porter taken in 1935. His face betrays years of hard work.

The co-operation of dockside teams was essential for the smooth handling of cargo. This did not always happen but this PLA Traffic Officer and his shed staff, including foremen on either side of him, seem happy to be together. The location is unknown.

Outside Head Office and the dock offices, women were found only in the warehouses.
These women are repacking tea at Commercial Road in the 1930s.

atrocious and dangerous conditions, turning many men old before their time. An official report in 1929 noted that 12 out of every 100 persons employed in UK docks received compensation for injury at work. Only miners and trawlermen had a higher accident rate. Ropes broke, bales were dropped, men were crushed. During a week-long smog in the early 1960s, one man at South West India Dock had a lucky escape. Working on the quayside, he inadvertently hooked a chain around his leg with a cargo set in the gloom, and was hoisted up above the concrete quay by the crane, dangling in mid-air. He was trembling like jelly when he was brought down to the ground.

For years dockers improvised their own safety equipment, such as the sacks, known as 'toe rags', they wore to protect their legs and feet when shovelling sugar. Even in the 1960s, overalls or duffle coats were available only if piece-work rates allowed them. Toe protectors for boots were offered at cost but rarely taken up. By the 1970s, with the Health and Safety At Work Act, 1974, and through the Docks Regulations, safety was being taken more seriously. There was better training, clothing and footwear, safer methods of handling cargo and safer working layouts. Although dockers were subject to popular criticism for stopping work at the drop of rain, they often worked through bitterly cold weather. One particularly weather-blasted part of the Royal Victoria Dock was known as 'Pneumonia Corner'. When it did rain, and dockers were stopped from working to prevent damage to the cargo, their earnings dropped.

For a long time amenities were often primitive. One man recalled how men working a cargo of lamp black had just one bucket of water between them. Toilets, without doors, consisted of a long board with holes cut in it over a trough, swilled through occasionally with water, even in the 1960s. Sometimes the foremen, entitled to a key to the office toilet through their status as Minor Staff, would lend it to the dockers, in the words of one man, 'to avoid the unpleasantness of the board plank and trough toilet'. One of these primitive latrines survived at the West India Docks Quadrangle Workshops until 1980, even

though dockers had enjoyed for many years the improvements provided by large modern amenity blocks, with their flushing toilets, showers, lockers and sometimes vending machines.

Mobile canteens were introduced for dock staff during the Second World War, lending their name to the term, 'mobiles', adopted by the dockers to describe their meal breaks. The tea they served was known colloquially as 'muggo' or 'mugger'. Later in the war these mobile units were supplemented by permanent canteens at 27 locations around the docks. The stylish, brick-built canteen at No. 7 Teak Shed, West India Docks, could serve 600 meals at one sitting.

Sometimes the dockers could turn their discomfort to their advantage. Jack Dash, the militant union leader, recalled how in the cold winter of 1947, when the rail-mounted quayside cranes were frozen and fires were kept burning beneath them to melt the ice from their wheels, a group of dockers, cold and hungry, noticed a hamper full of food and drink from an overseas government. It was addressed to Ernest Bevin, once the dockers' leader but then foreign secretary in the Labour government. Plundered, the hamper was re-packed and despatched with a card wishing Bevin a Happy Christmas.

Custom and practice in the docks included a certain level of pilfering. Shippers and others believed it was better to have minimal controlled pilfering. Contrary to popular perception, it was not confined to the dockers. Charles Connor's experience was that:

'the executive officer, the foreman, the cooper, the clerk and the labourer, they could all pilfer with a clear conscience. Yet they all considered taking anything out of the docks, however trifling, was stealing. So while the PLA did not countenance petty pilfering within the

docks, they turned a blind eye to it.
So dishonesty was kept within bounds.'

So, when a Scandinavian general cargo vessel came in, the dockers would sometimes take a little beer and fill their bread and butter from the fancy preserves, luncheon meat and tinned fish. At the West India Docks, where Scotch whisky was exported, the box in the middle of a cargo set might be filled with empty milk bottles, the dockers filling half-pint PLA mugs with whisky. There was always a bottle stashed away somewhere.

The tipple of illicit whisky was not the only drinking that went on in the docks. One tradition, known as 'having a waxer' or 'sucking the monkey', was enjoyed by dockers, staff and Customs and Excise officers. Strictly speaking, this applied only to those working in the vaults but visitors were often welcome and the process was regulated by the cooper, whose authority was respected and who ensured no one received drink in excess. The dockers would call for their first 'wet' at 8 am, with the request, 'Can I have a waxer, Mr Cooper?.' Until the 1970s every dock had its beer clubs (at the Millwall Docks they were known as 'beer cupboards'), often no more than a couple of stools and a keg of beer, where dockers slaked their thirst with a pint or two during their break. Smoking was frowned upon rather more than drinking, for obvious reasons, and was strictly prohibited in the docks. This did not prevent some of the men from having a smoke, but they did so only occasionally, and developed the habit of shielding their cigarette by turning it inwards, towards the

The PLA ambulance service, which was run by the PLA police force, shown here around 1930.

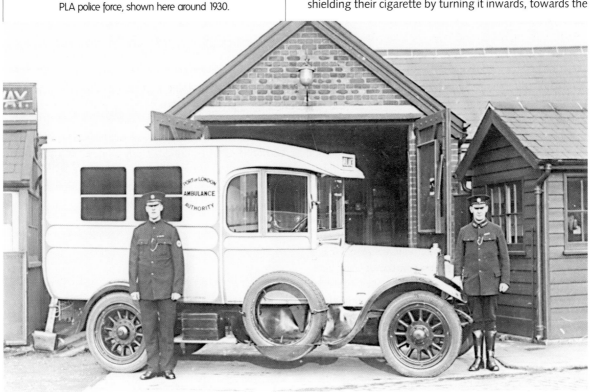

A river inspector, part of the Harbour Service, hails a PLA hopper barge in 1950.

palm of their hand. 'Cabbage!' was the shout that went up when a dock policeman was spotted and cigarettes had to be extinguished.

The etiquette of pilfering was complex. A PLA tally clerk would never knowingly allow the shipping clerk, or OST (Ocean Ship-owners' Tally Clerks), to fiddle the numbers on a cargo being discharged. There were unspoken limits that were not to be broken. A docker caught by the police risked losing his job, his card or, after the war, suspension by the Dock Labour Board and a spell in prison. PLA policemen on the dock gates carried out regular searches or 'rub downs'. One day in 1950 the police

constable on duty at a dock gate stopped and searched a hump-backed docker he did not recognise, only to discover the hump was false and hid a quantity of rationed chocolates and nylon stockings. A bigger problem was organised theft or fraud. Crooked lorry drivers might hide whisky behind the fascia of their cabs or line the inside of their doors with cigarettes. Merchants sometimes understated the weight of their cargoes to avoid paying higher charges, a dangerous thing to do when it resulted in cranes lifting goods heavier than was stated.

The dock police were an essential part of the Authority's organisation. As well as ensuring dock regulations and bye-laws were enforced, their activities ranged from tackling acts of minor vandalism by local children to foiling organised crime gangs stealing tractors for export

The Harbour Masters are key figures in ensuring the safe flow of traffic on the river. Here a Harbour Master boards a PLA launch at Woolwich pier in 1950

and apprehending seamen bringing drugs into the country.

They were absorbed within the PLA from the constabularies of the old dock companies in 1909. The latter had a reputation for being ineffective. The pay was poor, the calibre of recruits was dismal and there were too few of them. In the early years of the PLA, many constables were summarily dismissed, for being drunk on duty, smoking on duty or for taking articles out of the docks without a proper pass. Ship-owners and merchants were particularly concerned with the level of pilfering and supported a move to transfer the policing of the docks to the Metropolitan Police. Although the idea was rejected since the docks were private property and Tilbury was

outside the boundary of the Met, the London Chamber of Commerce reiterated the point that if the PLA was to retain a police force, it had to become more effective at controlling the loss of goods.

The PLA force was officially formed on 1 January 1910, under the command of a superintendent, J Cahill, formerly of the London and India Docks Police, with 10 inspectors, 26 sergeants, 386 constables, 18 firemen and 13 barge-searchers. The police also continued to run the ambulance service operating throughout the docks. In 1911, after the force had been reorganised, the first Chief Police Officer, E C Stuart-Baker, formerly with the Bengal and Assam police, was appointed. In 1913 a Criminal

Three PLA policemen engaged in their annual life-saving practice at West India Dock around 1930.

The motorcycle and radio telephone were hugely beneficial for the PLA police. Here a constable radios in from No.8 Gate, Royal Victoria Dock, in 1953.

Investigation Department was formed to boost the force's poor detection rates. A new headquarters building was opened close to the main entrance of West India Docks in 1914. By then, the force had increased in strength to 638, although half of them joined up with the services within a month of war being declared. In 1920, with a thousand men, the force was at its peak.

In that year, with the support of the shipping companies, the responsibilities of the force were extended to cover the inspection of ships, largely to control pilfering, with the creation of the 116-strong London Shipping Police. It was a successful but short-lived initiative. The Shipping Police were absorbed within the PLA force in 1932 after the shipping companies felt unable to continue their financial support. Within the docks and warehouses and within a radius of one mile beyond them, each officer had the same powers as those in any other police force. They were expected to live within nine miles of the dock gates and every one of them, like all other established dock staff, had to be able to swim – sadly, several policemen drowned while on duty over the years, usually in foggy weather.

As the docks declined, so the dock police force shrank in size. This policeman is on gate duty around 1980 at the passenger terminal at Tilbury, where the last of the dock police were based.

Conviction rates in general were high. Every year the number of cases under investigation steadily increased, rising from less than 500 in the mid-1930s to around 1,700 by the late 1940s. This period was marked by a steady decline in police numbers, which fell to 773 in 1927 and 490 in 1949. The force was seriously under-strength for much of the time as the PLA was compelled to make cutbacks, particularly during the inter-war years.

Poor pay and conditions remained a deterrent to recruitment, and the PLA had to make improvements at regular intervals to maintain parity with the Met. A review of the force in 1956 fixed the establishment at 584. By then, as well as foot patrols and guards at the dock gates, radio communications, motor-cycles and motor vehicles had all been adopted. In 1962 the jurisdiction of the force was extended beyond the one-mile range outside the docks by adding the right to 'pursue and follow' anywhere in the land.

By now, the force's detection rate had risen to around 60 per cent of the 2,000 cases investigated every year. Adapting to the container age, the force devised special search bays and mobile platforms, and new methods applied at Tilbury were taken up by ports around the UK and all over the world. But, as the docks declined, so too did the PLA police force. By the mid-1970s, when pilfering had been cut to just 0.003 per cent of the value of all goods handled, numbers were down to 300. Tilbury retained a small force of some 50 officers after the port was privatised in 1992.

In an age when many people found their recreation in group activities with colleagues and friends from work, the Authority, like other paternalistic employers, fostered a social spirit among its staff. Many activities were inherited by the PLA from the old dock companies, others were initiated within the new Authority. Sport was perpetually popular. The PLA Football Club was formed in 1912, playing at White Hart Lane, Tottenham, and won the London Commercial League in its first season. Competition to gain a place was intense, for each of the docks, from London and St Katharine to Tilbury, as well as head office, had their own teams. Many parts of the PLA had their own sports associations or clubs, from the Town Warehouses to the Tobacco Department. The PLA Sports Association, founded in 1913, had 3,000 members by 1939. In 1926 the Association moved to Cranbrook Rise in Ilford, with 30 acres of grounds and a purpose-built pavilion, designed by Edwin Cooper, the architect of the PLA's headquarters in Trinity Square. Football, cricket, hockey and lawn tennis were played. The rugby club was founded in 1927 and the badminton club the following year. The list was almost endless, from the golfing society to inter-departmental darts. One of the most remarkable sporting events was the swimming club's annual open-air gala, which in the early 1930s was held in the Millwall Cutting at the West India Dock, watched by as many as 4,000 spectators. The Ilford Sports Club, which fell on hard times during the Second World War, was revived when peace returned. A new Staff Club was formed in 1948, when it had more than 3,000 members. The club flourished during the 1950s but gradually fell into decline, although it lasted almost as long as the PLA ran the Port's enclosed docks. It closed in 1991, although bowls continued to be played there until the land was eventually sold.

Sport was just one of the activities enjoyed by staff. There was a literary and debating society, a dramatic society, an orchestral society and a male voice choir. There were clubs for bridge and chess, a camera circle and a horticultural society, sections for sailing and boating, motoring, angling and rifle shooting, even a scout club. Arts and Crafts Exhibitions were held annually from 1928 until 1968. In 1948 the exhibition was opened by Ernest Bevin, and in 1949 by the renowned painter, Dame Laura Knight. There were frequent dances and dinners, concerts in Rotherhithe Town Hall and plays at the Cripplegate Theatre. There were informal departmental trips, such as day trips down-river to Southend. During the 1930s these took place on board the popular paddle-steamers *Crested Eagle* and *Royal Eagle* – both these vessels later helped with the evacuation from Dunkirk and the former was sunk. After the war staff sailed on board the *Royal Sover-*

eign and *Royal Daffodil*. Presentations were made for weddings and retirements. The camaraderie which existed is clear from the affectionate nicknames by which many members of staff were remembered, from 'Convivial Bob' and 'The Bishop of Barking' to 'Uncle Bunkum' and the many 'Old' Bills, Georges, Freds and Jacks. Today the PLA still has some 3,000 pensioners, all with a continuing interest in the Authority, stemming from a working life with the PLA that often started on leaving school and ended with retirement.

The PLA always paid a disablement pension to its own 'perms' with more than 15 years' service, but this did not apply to the 'prefs' and certainly not to casual labour. The Authority had taken over existing pension schemes from the former dock companies and started its own staff pension scheme in 1917. It was quite usual for staff to be promoted one grade shortly before they retired, not just as a thank-you, but also to boost their pension.

The dockers fought for years for their own pension scheme. During the 1930s the PLA Board discussed the idea several times but decided there was little point unless similar schemes covered every other port. Finally, in 1953, when 22 other ports were operating the National Dock Labour Scheme, the PLA accepted the principle of a contributory scheme for 'perms', initiated

There were many active sports teams within the PLA. Here is the PLA Staff Club Darts Section Team B in 1951.

The staff of today's PLA include river inspectors, Michael Scarce, Ian Yarton and Paul Arnold, with the Houses of Parliament behind.

through legislation in 1958, This also applied to all other so-called 'unestablished' staff but was overtaken in 1961 by a nationwide pension scheme, covering all registered dockers, when 90 per cent of those eligible applied for membership. Implementation came too late. Within a few years there were too many dockers for the work available. Pensions from the national scheme were insufficient to encourage them to give up their jobs without a greater financial incentive, ultimately making severance much more costly for the Authority.

Marine staff have been almost as diverse as those working in the docks, from harbour masters and hydrographers to masters and mates of the dredgers and hoppers. The last of the dredgermen left the PLA in 1991 when the work was contracted out. Many of the experienced professionals employed in the marine service have come from the merchant marine or the Royal Navy, using their expertise to develop areas within the PLA such as VTS.

Among the most recent skilled personnel to join the Authority are the pilots. Today the PLA employs some 78 sea pilots and 12 river pilots, three of whom are bridge pilots, guiding special cargo vessels through the London bridges. All of them are master mariners, many with experience of command. With four pilot stations, at

PLA pilot Dave Hocking (right) guides HMS *Bulwark* up the Thames during its visit to Greenwich in November 2007.

Gravesend, Sheerness, Ramsgate and Harwich, the Authority's pilots carry out around 12,000 operations every year, taking vessels from the smallest coaster to the largest container vessel through the shoals and channels of the tidal Thames. Piloting a major container vessel up the Thames to Tilbury takes little short of five hours to accomplish. Although pilots are assisted by the latest GPS technology, none of this displaces their traditional skills, as they keep a wary eye on the wind and tides, ship speed and visibility. The PLA pilots play an immense part in keeping the tidal Thames safe. Many of them now take turns to supervise the Port Control Centre for a shift as Duty Port Controller.

Equally invaluable are the support services offered for many years by the PLA's marine staff, from diving and salvage to underwater inspections and the inspection and licensing of vessels using the river. Buoys and bridge navigation lights are all maintained by PLA staff, they mark obstructions in the river and lay out temporary markings for major river events, for which they also act as marshals. Without the PLA divers, work on London's bridges, the maintenance of lock gates and sluices and the assessment of damage to vessels on the river would be impossible. While the dock police may no longer be the PLA's responsibility, the security of the Port

The PLA tradition of developing employees continues with its marine trainee programme. This is Sarah Kember, recruited in 2008.

as a whole remains a prime consideration for the Authority's port security staff, who work with a wide array of other organisations in keeping emergency plans for the Port up to date.

The PLA has revived apprenticeships within the Authority, focusing on the skills needed to sustain its work. Recently the Authority recognised that it could no longer rely on traditional sources of recruitment in a world short of experienced seamen, and, with the recruitment of the first marine trainee in 2007, began training the Harbour Masters of the future.

Many staff would echo the words of Bill Bean, still working for the Authority after nearly 40 years: 'The PLA is our life … the river runs through our veins … it's an organisation that I love working for … there's a lot of goodwill towards the PLA from the staff'. His is not an isolated view. To take another example, Bob Aspinall, who spent most of his working life with the Authority, recalled that it was 'a great place … it was a happy ship … working on the river, in the docks, with cargo, created a special kind of relationship … loyalty to the PLA was taken for granted'. It is this spirit, fostered by the PLA for a hundred years, which has helped to make working for the Authority an enriching experience for so many.

The *Galloper* is the latest addition to the PLA's fleet of hydrographic vessels, deriving greater operational flexibility from its shallow draft.

4 PRESENT AND FUTURE 1992 ONWARDS

Since 1992 the PLA has concentrated principally on its core responsibility, the safety of navigation on the tidal Thames. The sale of Tilbury, home of the Authority's sole remaining cargo-handling operations, prompted this change. It also ushered in a period that has seen the PLA re-establish its financial stability, handle the shock of a major terminal closure and become progressively closer to its many customers and stakeholders along the river. After a hundred years, the Authority enters its second century working in support of exciting developments along the river, such as the new London Gateway Port.

The PLA was already changing as an organisation before the privatisation of Tilbury. The stewardship of Sir Brian Kellett, who stepped down at the end of 1992, had paved the way for the Authority to focus entirely upon the river. As well as encouraging the privatisation of Tilbury, Kellett had split the PLA into three divisions (River Division, Property Division and Port of Tilbury). With an eye to the future, he had also recruited David Jeffery from outside the organisation in 1986 as Chief Executive, River, and welcomed Sir Brian Shaw, with long experience in shipping, to the Board in 1987.

David Jeffery and Sir Brian Shaw worked together closely on the PLA's river committee, which Sir Brian chaired. In 1993, Shaw appropriately became Chairman of the PLA, now focused on what had been the River Division, while Jeffery became the first Chief Executive of the restructured Authority.

The contributions that they and their colleagues made to changing the outlook and performance of the PLA continued under their successors, Simon Sherrard, another very experienced shipping industry executive, who took over as Chairman in 2001, Steve Cuthbert,

The PLA's Port Control Centre in Gravesend oversees shipping on the river around the clock throughout the year.
Photo shows: Vessel Traffic Services Officer, Matthew Mays.

Chief Executive from 1999 until 2004, and Richard Everitt, Chief Executive from 2005.

Those PLA corporate staff based at Tilbury who remained within the Authority moved, sometimes after short stays in temporary office space, to work at the PLA's new bases on the other side of the river at London River House in Gravesend and nearby Denton Wharf. For many, this was just the latest in a series of relocations which had seen them move gradually downriver from central London or the enclosed docks. London River House was purpose-built as the main PLA office on land next to the existing Port Control Centre. Costing some £3 million (£4.5 million in today's prices), it was built between 1991 and 1992, with staff moving in during September 1992.

There and at the London head office, one of the immediate changes to be faced, following the separation from Tilbury, was that of achieving financial certainty. It should be remembered that the PLA was still paying for the historic costs of the National Dock Labour Scheme, costs which had led to the entire demise of other port authorities, such as the Mersey Docks and Harbour Board. The government agreed that the PLA should no longer be liable for the repayment of any outstanding balance of the grants it had received. This commitment was given in

return for the proceeds from the long-term, planned disposal of PLA property assets that were no longer relevant to the operations of the 'new' PLA. Geoff Ellis, then the PLA's Chief Financial Officer, oversaw the implementation of this plan, from 1 January 1994.

In some quarters, concerns were voiced that high Port dues disadvantaged commerce to and from the Port. Against this backdrop of some commercial tension, Tilbury nevertheless went from strength to strength. The ships did not stop coming in or out and the tonnage of cargoes through the Port quickly returned to levels not seen since the early 1970s.

Traditionally, the PLA had always covered rising costs simply by increasing charges made to Port users. After the privatisation of Tilbury, it became clear that this approach would have to change. A start was made under David Jeffery, through the overdue rationalisation of the formidably complex list of widely differing dues and charges. For some years, there was a standstill on increasing Port charges. These changes encouraged existing operators to remain in the Port. So too did the lower charges arising from the reorganisation of the Thames pilots, as they moved from Trinity House's operational management into the employment of the PLA, a move

guided by Sir Brian Shaw. After the increasingly successful privatisation of Tilbury and with an improving world
economy, trade to and from the Port revived. Cargoes
reached a peak of 56 million tonnes in the mid-1990s, and
have since averaged around 52 million tonnes annually.
London is thus the second largest UK port, regularly vying
for this position with another major oil and chemical port,
Tees and Hartlepool. The UK's largest port has been
Grimsby & Immingham since 2000, the year after the
closure of the Shell Haven oil refinery on the Thames. Oil
continues to be a bedrock of Thames-side trade. Nonethe-
less, in 1998, London achieved a record 29.5 million
tonnes of non-fuel cargo.

The growth in trade recorded in 1998 was significant, for in the same year the closure of the Shell Haven

Sir Brian Shaw, Chairman of the PLA from 1993 until 2000,
was instrumental in helping the Authority adjust to its new role
after the privatisation of Tilbury.

oil refinery was announced by the Anglo-Dutch company
Royal Dutch Shell. This decision gave the PLA financial
pause for thought. Closure of the refinery would deprive
the Authority of the revenue from around seven million
tonnes of cargo landed at Shell Haven each year –
accounting for around 15 per cent of the PLA's revenue
income – a staggering amount to lose at one stroke.

The closure of Shell Haven refinery, except for the
smaller-scale bitumen and aviation fuel business, which
remained on the site, meant the Authority risked losing
money from 2000 onwards. Its response addressed all
the elements within its control, including bearing down on
staffing and office costs, seeking efficiencies and better
working practices throughout. The PLA also took the
important immediate step, together with Shell, of actively
marketing the former oil refinery site, which was able to
accommodate some of the world's largest ships. This initiative ultimately resulted in P&O Ports bringing forward
plans to develop a major new container port, with an
adjacent business park on the site. The complex approval
process was lengthy but the new London Gateway Port is
now being developed by DP World, who took over P&O
Ports in 2006. Approval for the project was received from
the government on 30 May 2007. A Harbour Empower-
ment Order, formally creating London Gateway Port, was
made a year later.

While this positive development was some way
off, and in the immediate aftermath of the Shell decision,
the new PLA Chairman, Simon Sherrard, and new Chief
Executive, Steve Cuthbert, were clear that the Authority
could no longer rely on returning to a time of automati-
cally increasing charges above the rate of inflation. The
PLA had to concentrate on achieving a financial surplus,
by offering its customers better services more cost-effec-
tively. This focus on service became an established theme
embraced throughout the PLA. This has been developed
most recently as a result of action taken following a review
in 2007 of how easy and effective the Port was to use.

This concentration on customers and their needs
helped to change the way in which major commercial

operators within the Port saw the PLA. Nevertheless the Authority still had to address concerns by the major Port customers that charges levied on their operations helped subsidise expenditure the PLA necessarily had to make in the middle and upper reaches of the river. In fact, these operations were self-financing, largely due to river rents levied in this area, a situation that improved progressively through increased property values in London.

The sale of Tilbury docks also marked a further reduction in the PLA's direct influence over trade and development on the river and in the Port. In its place, the Authority became increasingly skilled at working in partnership with the many organisations interested in the river, from terminal operators and rowing clubs to environmental groups and fellow regulators.

In advance of the partnership approach so firmly embedded today, the PLA increased its active promotion of the Port abroad. This endeavour, developed under the chairmanship of Sir Brian Shaw, was a continuation of the PLA's tradition of promoting London. Echoing the promotional efforts at venues around the world between the two World Wars, it was now particularly necessary to support the development of trade. The main aim was to counter the common perception among those beyond the Port community, and particularly overseas, that the Port had closed with the last of the old docks.

The leading role taken by the PLA in promoting the Port as a whole overseas complemented the individual marketing work of the Port's commercial operators. But as the commercial operators became more sophisti-

The Thames is a haven for recreational activity - here kayaking just downstream of Chelsea Harbour.

cated and effective in their own marketing, these marketing efforts were reduced from 2005. Instead, the PLA moved towards engaging with a broader range of stakeholders, throughout London, together with the development of more direct links with established commercial interests, on issues related to the services they received from the PLA, as well as other regulatory matters.

This shift of emphasis in marketing and communication was possible partly because of the work already done by the PLA among river users and within the capital to clear up misconceptions about the Authority. Sir Brian Shaw nurtured this sense of partnership by cultivating influential figures from across the capital, striving to ensure they were left better informed about the Authority and developments on the river. All this contributed to a greater understanding of the continued importance of the Port and the river, and of the Authority's position on key issues.

One important issue that emerged with the growing attraction of waterside sites for residential development was the safeguarding of existing wharves for commercial use. Government was slow at first to appreciate the importance of these sites but, by the end of the Conservative administration in 1997, government depart-

ments were working more closely with the PLA, identifying more than 30 sites for safeguarding. A close relationship was quickly established with the first Mayor of London, Ken Livingstone, on his election in 2000. The Mayor's responsibilities included executive responsibility for strategic planning, including the river wharves, and the promotion of passenger and goods transport on the Thames. Livingstone shared the PLA's vision for the river and strongly believed that the Thames had the potential to help relieve road congestion in the capital.

In 2004, the Mayor's London Plan included strong protection for the 29 safeguarded wharves located upstream of the Thames Barrier at Woolwich. A further London report in 2005, undertaken in conjunction with the PLA's Planning Department, was accepted by the government, which listed 25 wharves upstream of the Thames Barrier and 25 downstream of the Barrier for protection, covering various locations along the river between Fulham and Erith. 'There is no shortage of operators,' the Authority reported in 2006, 'keen to start up port-related

> The Thames is the UK's busiest inland freight waterway, moving over two million tonnes of materials every year and keeping many tens of thousands of lorries off the capital's busy roads.

PLA pilot Ed Hadnett boards a container ship off the Kent coast. Pilots guide over 12,000 ships in and out of the Port each year.

operations on these prime riverside sites.' When the modified policy was tested in the Peruvian Wharf planning inquiry of 2007, the PLA joined with the Mayor of London in fighting plans for a mixed-use, but predominantly residential, development on the safeguarded wharf. The Secretary of State agreed with the Planning Inspector that planning permission should be refused.

Five private wharves still operate in the upper river: Cringle Wharf and Cringle Dock, Battersea; Comleys Wharf, Fulham; Pier Wharf, and Smugglers Way, Wandsworth. The Mayor was right – over 190,000 lorry deliveries are saved, every year, by using the river to move cargo between wharves solely within the Greater London area.

Safety on the river had become the subject of considerable public and media attention during Lord Justice Clarke's inquiry into river safety, which was published in 2000. The PLA's enthusiastic and full support for that inquiry and for the Marchioness Formal Investigation that followed added to its reputation for promoting and regulating navigational safety on the tidal Thames. One important change arising from the inquiry was the introduction on the tidal river in January 2002 of a new Search and Rescue operation, with four RNLI boats based at four new stations, Teddington, Chiswick, Tower and Gravesend. Safety has been enhanced by the installation of advanced Vessel Traffic Services systems at the Port Control

Shipment of bulk materials in barges continues to be important on the Thames.

The ship's bridge simulator in Gravesend is used for pilot training and assessing proposed new developments on the river. Photo shows PLA Pilot, Nick Benson.

Centre and the Thames Barrier Navigation Control Centre. The mandatory carriage of Automatic Identification Systems (AIS) has also improved safety. Required on ocean going ships from 2005, carriage of the specially developed Thames AIS derivative was required on larger passenger craft, smaller commercial vessels and all tugs and tows in central London from mid-2007. This allowed every vessel on the river to identify others and establish their proximity.

The PLA records and reviews navigational incidents using its Safety Management System (SMS), an operation under the control of the Chief Harbour Master. The SMS provides the formal framework through which the PLA manages safety on the river, identifying risks and how they should be removed or kept to a minimum. The

installation of a ship pilotage and control simulator at Gravesend in 2003 has proved invaluable for training pilots and testing conditions for proposed new berths for all manner of ships. The PLA is also eager to improve the way it forecasts the increase in traffic into and out of the river, for this has a direct impact on the demand for pilots, each of whom requires four to five years of training and experience before they can obtain their Class 1 qualification.

Such is the topography of the estuary that the banks of the lower reaches of the Thames are lined with areas of legally protected natural habitat. Equally the

Over half the sand and gravel used in London comes in by sea, taken from approved reserves in the English Channel. The PLA actively encourages the use of the river for freight.

upper river has its share of sensitive areas, with Sites of Special Scientific Interest (SSSIs) such as Syon Park protected as an unchanging riverside environment.

Striking the right balance between recreation, commerce and the marine environment has become one of the PLA's major roles. Often, all three can co-exist quite happily – Richard Everitt remembered his first experience of this equilibrium when, shortly after his arrival, he found himself on a snowy January evening at a commercial jetty near Dartford, where close by on the mudbanks a mass of wildfowl was feeding at low tide.

Under its role as the conservation and licensing authority for any structures in, under or over the river, and as the owner of the majority of the tidal river bed and foreshore, the PLA has committed itself to the joint objectives of protecting the environment and pursuing sustainable development. This duty is the more challenging as PLA has oversight of dredging the river and how the dredged material is handled, without detriment to the river or riverside sites.

To develop a greater understanding of the impact of dredging upon the ecology of the river, the PLA initiated a pioneering study into the effects of dredging in the vicinities of the conservation sites within the Thames estuary. Among the main findings of the report, supported by conservation bodies, was the importance of retaining clean sediment within the estuary to maintain key bird-feeding habitats. Joined by professionals from the Environment Agency, the PLA commissioned work to extend its standard mathematical model of the Thames's

One of the last of the Concorde fleet passes the
Palace of Westminster in 2004.

tidal and fluvial flow, to produce a more accurate and consistent aid for those seeking to carry out developments in or near the river. Already strong links with the RSPB have further developed with a Memorandum of Understanding signed between the two organisations in 2008, under which RSPB will use its expertise to help the PLA develop its Conservation Management Framework. RSPB and PLA already worked together closely including at Rainham marshes where the RSPB is managing the site's vast and diverse fauna and heritage in concert with ongoing land uses, including the lagoons used for disposal of materials dredged from the river.

In support of government and London initiatives, the PLA also encourages the increased use of the river as a preferred alternative wherever possible for the carriage of goods and passengers. This concept was

demonstrated, among other notable occasions, when the river was used to carry individual sections of the Millennium Wheel, the fuselage of a Concorde aeroplane on its last journey, and later the movement of eight giant fermenting tanks from the Guinness brewery at Park Royal to Tilbury for onward shipment by sea to Dublin. As preparations began for the 2012 Olympic Games in London, the PLA joined with other authorities and commercial entities to make the case for the Thames to be considered an integral part of the transport proposals for the Games.

As an organisation now collectively focused on effective and safe use of the tidal Thames, the PLA has actively fostered better relationships with a wide range of

The ro-ro trades flourish on the Thames. These vessels are seen close by the Queen Elizabeth II Bridge in 2008.

RICHMOND LOCK & WEIR

On the upper river, the PLA continues to operate a working monument of Victorian engineering. Richmond Lock – which actually comprises a weir, a lock, boat slips and footbridges – was built by the Thames Conservancy in 1894 to the designs of F G M Stoney. The Lock had its origins in the removal of the old medieval London Bridge in 1832. The piers of the bridge were supported on 17 massive and closely spaced timber and rubble 'starlings', which partially dammed the flow of the river. When the starlings were removed, the flow and tidal regime of the river changed. This, together with increased dredging, resulted in the lowering of water levels above Richmond. Stoney's solution was to provide a weir – consisting of 32-ton steel lifting sluice gates in the three bridge arches – between the large barge lock (on the Surrey side) and the slipway for small boats (on the Middlesex side). For around two hours on either side of high tide, the gates are raised and boats can pass directly through the bridge arches.

For the rest of the time, the gates are lowered and boats have to use the lock and boat slips. When the gates are down, the water above the Lock is maintained at 1.72 metres above Chart Datum. The operation of the sluices varies during periods of both drought and high river flow. In the early 1990s, the PLA undertook a £4 million (£6 million in today's prices) refurbishment of the Lock, which is Grade II* listed. The work was completed in time for the centennial celebrations of the structure in 1994. Every November, the sluices are raised for a three-week period to allow for essential works. During this time the water level above the Lock is reduced and the riverbanks exposed. This allows scientists to check for invasive alien marine species such as Chinese mitten crabs and zebra mussels which threaten the conservation of native species.

The official naming of river patrol boat *Chelsea* alongside at Richmond Lock in 2007.

river users. Progress and success with this initiative has been particularly marked in the upper river, where a perception had developed that the PLA was indifferent to the river's conservation and the needs of its users in that area.

A more open management culture developed throughout this time. This process crystallised in Richard Everitt's introduction of public meetings along the length of the river, giving river users and community members alike unfettered access to the PLA's top management and navigation team and the scope for direct consultation on a wide range of issues within their interest. This bold liaison was a further step to tackle the PLA's challenge that Sir Brian Shaw summarised as 'to promote and facilitate use of the Thames and reconcile the often conflicting interests of those who use it'.

It took time to convince river users that the PLA was changing, with great contributions from the Chief Harbours Masters, Bruce Richardson, who served from

1994 to 2006 and now his successor, David Snelson. The openness and willingness of the PLA to engage in debate with river users gradually won their respect. The immediate fruits of this endeavour have been most evident in the transformation of the PLA's up-river operation. Here, a new Code of Practice for Rowing, developed in conjunction with the rowing community, has been introduced, backed by prizes for rowing clubs demonstrating keenest commitment to enhancing safety. New low-wash patrol boats, especially designed for operations in the shallower water of the upper district, were brought into service and a River Manager, with experience of and many contacts within the rowing and leisure communities, was appointed to be the PLA's first manager 'on the ground', between Putney and Teddington.

London plays host to regular visits from Royal Navy vessels. Here HMS *Ark Royal* passes through the Thames Barrier in 2007.

Safety, environment and the economy sums up the modern PLA's approach to its business. It is an organisation that has used its statutory role as a regulator, its breadth of managerial and specialist corporate knowledge, and its flexibility to adapt, to transform itself into an effective facilitator, certainly making sure that the regulations are met but doing as much as possible to help all river users go about their business or leisure activities and developments in safety and efficiently.

The PLA's Strategic Framework Summary, published in 2007, sets out the core purpose of the organisation as follows: 'to be the leader in the management of port navigation services and the marine environment of the tidal River Thames, promoting its safe and sustainable

use for trade, transport, leisure and events.'

The steps towards achieving this purpose include sound financial management; the organisation's navigational safety management system; its understanding and stewardship of the environment; the provision of quality services; its support for the sustainable development of trade on the tidal Thames; direct support for safeguarding essential infrastructure; and active engagement, by managers and staff, with stakeholders.

As shippers increasingly used GPS techniques to track their cargoes and containers, traditional port management techniques were no longer enough to meet their expectations of avoiding delay. The PLA took the initiative and the 2007 'End to End' review of shipping

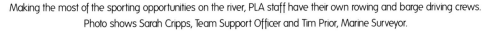

Making the most of the sporting opportunities on the river, PLA staff have their own rowing and barge driving crews.
Photo shows Sarah Cripps, Team Support Officer and Tim Prior, Marine Surveyor.

customers' experience of using the Port identified further areas for improvement, which are now being actively investigated and pursued. As a major step towards providing a 'seamless' service for ships entering or leaving the Thames, a computer-based port-wide booking system (PISCES) is being introduced. Working in concert with ships' agents and other interests, this approach and system will enable the simultaneous coordination of all the information needed to service a ship – from pilots to tugs. Pilotage, the critical service underpinning safety and efficiency in the Port, is also being boosted with operational refinements and through additional, focused dialogue with customers. Through this, the Authority is developing a closer knowledge of customers' plans and requirements. This will enable it to improve its ability to deliver key services, such as pilotage – where employee training to full competence takes a particularly long time – with greater assurance and in a timely manner.

With the development of PISCES, the PLA is adding to the suite of information systems that aid the smooth running of the Port. The computerised port information system, known as PACE and first devised in the 1980s, and the river information system (POLARIS), which announces a vessel's arrival in the Thames and tracks it to the berth and away, have both been constantly modernised. This ensures they give users continued improvement in performance and cater for emerging changes in transportation modes and patterns.

The PLA's driftwood operations gather more than 400 tonnes of rubbish from the river every year.
Photo shows Danny Wade, Harbour Service Coxwain and Neil Jeffery, Driftwood Skipper.

The investment in PISCES is one example of the ways in which the PLA directs its financial resources to deliver its commitments. The year 2008 saw the completion of the latest phase of the deepening of Princes Channel, which has now become one of the busiest approaches to the Thames. The first major 'capital' dredge in the Port for over 40 years, this project helped maintain the Port's attractiveness by giving more ships access to a shorter, simpler, safer route to and from berths along the riverbank.

In line with the PLA's general and navigational safety commitment, financial support has been given to domestic passenger vessel operators to facilitate the introduction of the new Thames AIS safety equipment onto vessels working in central London. In addition, substantial funds are invested regularly in maintaining and enhancing the Authority's radar and vessel traffic services systems, to improve the level of service and to deliver greater safety on the river.

The PLA's marine services support operations are based at Denton Wharf. Redevelopment of this strategic site commenced in 2001. The jetty was demolished and rebuilt, with a heavy-lift jetty crane and the only 70-tonne boat lift on the river, to serve both the PLA's fleet and the wider river community on a commercial basis.

The PLA, seen represented here at the Thames Festival, is actively involved with the whole of the river community.

The latest development at Denton, Marine House, was completed in 2006. The base for management of the PLA's Marine Services, Marine Engineering and stores, and also home to ship towage operator Svitzer's operations on the Thames, it forms a core of marine expertise on the river.

Resources afloat also continue to benefit from investment. The organisation is standardising its fleet of patrol and pilotage launches, introducing more economical, carbon-friendly twin-hulled vessels for the Middle and Lower Districts. This move will draw on the successful introduction of the new low-wash launches now in use in the Upper District, which combine better operational performance with reduced impact on the environment.

These direct and substantial investments of initiative, money and resource are matched with a drive for continuous improvement across the whole organisation's performance. This endeavour is evident through the certification to international standards of the PLA's quality and environmental management systems. In the management of its marine activities, all the PLA's staff on the river, from the crews of the harbour service launches to the crews of the driftwood collection boats and salvage ships, have been brought together as a single, more flexible team. Environmental performance has been improved by simple

The PLA manages the lights and buoys within its operational limits. This is the Sea Reach 3 Buoy.

Tilbury, which was for over 80 years a core part of the PLA, today handles over ten million tonnes of cargo a year.

London's container and other unitised trades broke the two million TEU barrier for the first time in 2007.

measures, such as the fitting of movement-sensitive lights throughout the PLA's main operational bases. The more complex, such as funding computer modelling and towing tank tests to identify the best hull shapes to save fuel and minimise wash, also have their part to play.

Inevitably, there have been periods of tension between the PLA and its many partner organisations and other stakeholder groups – a regulator can rarely be every one's friend all of the time. The transition from the traditional local licensing of Watermen and Lightermen on the Thames to a national scheme promoted and overseen by the UK Maritime and Coastguard Agency is a case in point. The PLA's commitment has been to continue the dialogue and to work to resolve differences over time. In the case of the change in licensing regime, the Authority set up a special fund to support enhanced training through the transition to the new regime.

LONDON GATEWAY PORT

The construction of London Gateway Port on the north bank of the Thames in Essex is the most significant development in the Port of London in over a century.

The DP World project involves the development of a major new deep-water facility at the former Shell Haven oil refinery site in Thurrock, Essex. Its unique advantages are the combination of a world-class port and the largest logistics and business park in the UK, side by side, just 20 miles from London and the major markets in the south east of England.

Many of the PLA's duties, responsibilities and qualities are exemplified by its contribution to this enormous project, which has the potential for doubling trade through the Port. Operational and navigational safety is a paramount consideration, since the largest container vessels in the world will be able to berth there. Environmental considerations, given the PLA's duty to conservation, are crucial as London Gateway is located in a sensitive area of the estuary. As the development will take place within the Authority's waters, the PLA will work to ensure these safety and environmental aspects are safeguarded through, for example, hydrographic surveying and tidal works approvals. At the same time, the PLA will also work to ensure that the traffic of vessels into and out of the UK's second-largest port is unimpeded, while the major works are under way.

This new, world-class port will demand world-class support services. Through its efficient provision of pilots, harbour services and vessel traffic control, the PLA will ensure these needs are met for London Gateway, in the longer term, as it does today for all other Port users.

Computer generated illustration of DP World's London Gateway Port. (DP World)

The PLA regularly checks the river bed, using the latest hydrographic survey equipment. Photo shows Rob Howard, Hydrographic Surveyor.

One hundred years after the PLA was created, it is legitimate to ask whether the Authority has achieved what it was asked to do and whether it still continues to do so.

For the years immediately after it was established, the simple answer must be an emphatic 'yes'. The PLA brought discipline to the management of the world's largest Port and ensured it was properly equipped for the future. In later years, the emerging challenges, whether labour relations, trade patterns or technological changes, were ones that the organisation's founding fathers may never have anticipated. Throughout the last century, to meet the evolving challenges, the organisation balanced a complex range of disciplines including marine navigation, engineering, trade and financial management against the various and disparate demands which it encountered. In

general, the overall result was one of continued success, albeit sometimes gradual, irrespective of the magnitude of the challenges that beset the organisation, the city and country which it served.

The result, after a hundred years of change, is an organisation of some 360 staff, considerably less than the 11,000 when the PLA was formed. But this smaller number, and a turnover of £40 million, belies the national and regional contribution made by the Authority. Like many of its staff, such as the pilots and VTS operators, without whom traffic on the river would come to a halt,

PLA's upgraded Vessel Traffic System at Gravesend was officially opened by Bill O'Neil, Secretary General of the International Maritime Organisation in October 1998. Photo shows (l-r): Bruce Richardson Chief Harbour Master (1994 to 2006), Bill O'Neil, David Jeffery, Chief Executive (1993 to 1999), Juan Kelly, PLA Vice Chairman (1993-1998) and then Gravesham MP, Chris Pond.

the PLA undoubtedly plays the part of the unsung and unseen hero, in a nation that still relies for 95 per cent of its imports upon the sea. The PLA oversees the busiest inland waterway in the UK in terms of freight movements, ensuring that the 30,000 movements made by commercial vessels and the 200,000 movements made by leisure vessels every year, plus more than 50 major events, from the revived Thames sailing barge match to the Oxford and Cambridge Boat Race, all take place in conditions of the best possible safety.

Today the PLA also remains a unifying force within the UK's second-largest port. The wharves and terminals that make up the Port handle over 50 million tonnes of cargo a year, to and from more than 80 countries around the world. Research commissioned by the PLA in 2003 showed that the Port contributes towards

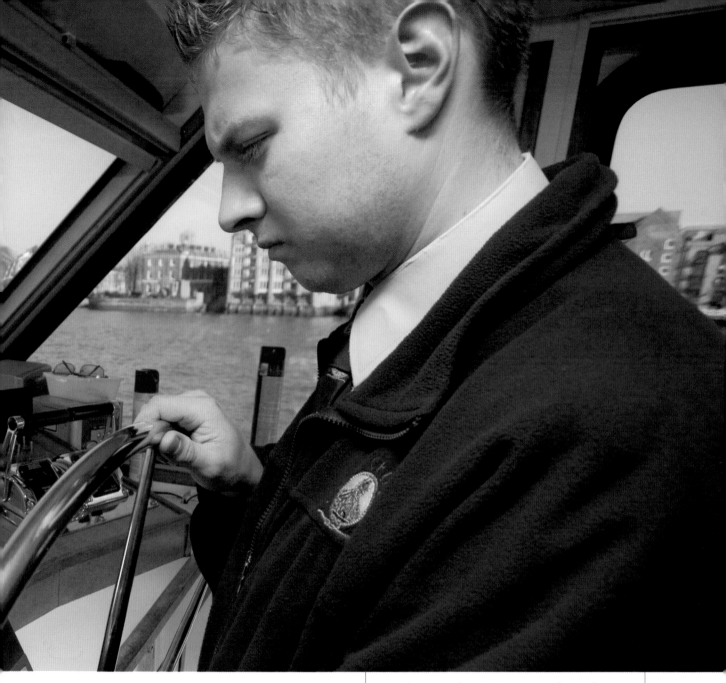

A crew member entering passenger data into the Thames Automatic Identification System on board a passenger vessel on the Thames.

the employment of more than 30,000 people and the generation of almost £3.5 billion within the regional economy. Going forward, the prospects for London's trade and its continued success in the future look most promising. Over 50 per cent of the UK's manufacturing and trading activity is located within a two-hour drive of the Port's main terminals, benefiting a rather larger proportion of the UK's population.

Tilbury, for over 80 years at the heart of the PLA, draws on this geographical strength and continues to flourish as a major centre for cargo handling and distribution. Developments planned there over the coming years are expected to include a new riverside ro-ro berth and further expansion of container capacity. This will complement the major development of London Gateway which is set to radically transform London's capabilities. Other projects which underline the continued vibrancy of the Port include the planned new clean coal-fired power station at Tilbury and the expected growth in the use of the river for moving materials linked to projects such as the Olympics, Thames Tideway Tunnel and Crossrail.

The breadth of expertise within the PLA remains remarkable: from boat crews and specialist engineering managers and staff to hydrographers, harbour masters

and town planners. Their levels of knowledge and skill, their sheer passion for the most famous river in the world, and their commitment to the work of the PLA stand out among their peers in each of their specialisations and professions. And the PLA, a smaller, more informal organisation, now liberated from its past, focused on the future, has retained the ethos of public service on which it was founded.

Out of all this, strengthened through a century of service, is the bond between the PLA and its people with the Thames, London and its Port. After a hundred years, the PLA remains a vital part of the future of all three.

A bulk carrier making its way up the Thames, having passed under the Queen Elizabeth II Bridge.

CHRONOLOGY

Year

1197 Conservancy powers granted to the Lord Mayor and Corporation of London

1798 West India Committee funds a River Constabulary

1799 Act for the Improvement of the Port of London establishes powers to appoint a Harbour Master and to establish a mooring chains service

1802 West India Dock opened

1805 London Dock opened

1806 East India Dock opened

1807 Emergence of Surrey Commercial Docks system

1828 St Katharine Dock opened

1855 Victoria Dock opened

1857 Thames Conservancy formed

1862 First cargo of oil arrived in the Thames

1864 St Katharine Dock Company amalgamated with London Dock Company to form the London and St Katharine Dock Company

1868 Millwall Dock opened

1870 South West India Dock opened

1878 *The Princess Alice* disaster

1880 Royal Albert Dock opened; Victoria Dock becomes Royal Victoria Dock

1886 Tilbury Dock opened

1888 East and West India Dock Company and London and St Katharine Company form the London and India Joint Docks Committee

1889 Strike for 'the dockers' tanner'

1894 Richmond Lock & Weir opened

1894 Thames Conservancy Consolidation Act

1900 Royal Commission established to enquire into the Port of London

1901 London and India Docks Company formed

1902 Royal Commission report recommends creation of a Port Authority

1908 Port of London Authority created through the Port of London Act

1909 Port of London Authority established

1909 LCC hands over river piers to PLA

1910 PLA employs 11,297 people

1910 PLA police force established

1911 Dock strike leads to the Devonport Agreement

1912 Construction of King George V Dock begins

1912 Lightermen's strike leads to general dock strike

1912 London overtaken by Hamburg as the world's leading port

1912 PLA FC formed

1913 Construction of Head Office, Trinity Square, begins

1913 PLA Sports Association formed

1913 Robert Philipson, first General Manager, retired

1916 Shell Haven oil refinery opened

1917 Silvertown explosion

1917 Staff pension scheme started

1920 Shaw Inquiry into dock labour

1921 King George V Dock opened

1921 Port of New York Authority founded, based on PLA model

1922 Coryton oil refinery opened

1922 David Owen appointed General Manager

1922 Trinity Square Head Office opened

1924 Maclean Enquiry into dock labour

1925 Deepening of Yantlet Channel completed

1926 General Strike

1926 *London Mammoth* commissioned

1926 PLA Sports Association moves to new club at Ilford

1926 Quebec Dock completed in Surrey Commercial Docks

1927 PLA RFC formed

1928 First annual arts and crafts exhibition held

1929 PLA publicity department established

1929 Tilbury – new entrance lock completed

1930 Tilbury passenger landing stage opened

1931 First public dock and river cruises operated by the PLA

1934 Silvertown Way completed

1936 Reconstruction of Royal Victoria Dock started

1938 Douglas Ritchie appointed General Manager

1938 PLA film, *City of Ships*, made

1940 First bombs fall on the docks on 7 September

1940 Salvage department established

1941 National Dock Labour Corporation formed and compulsory registration introduced for all dockers

1944 Tilbury Hotel destroyed by bombing

1946   East India Import Dock closed
1946   First ro-ro services in the Port commence
      at Tilbury
1946   Theo Williams appointed General Manager
1947   National Dock Labour Scheme established
1947   PLA mechanisation committee formed
1948   Leslie Ford appointed General Manager
1948   PLA introduces short-wave radio communication
1949   Deep-water berths created at West India
      Import Dock
1949   First bulk sugar cargo discharged in the Port
1951   First mechanised export berth opened at South
      West India Quay
1951   PLA film, *Waters of Time*, made
1953   PLA takes delivery of last steam railway engine
1955   PLA introduces radar
1955   Rotterdam overtakes London in importance
      as a port
1957   Modernisation of Millwall Docks begins
1957   Tilbury passenger terminal (No. 1 Berth) opened
1958   Pension scheme started for permanent
      dock workers
1959   First cargo of liquid natural gas arrives in
      the Thames
1959   Thames Navigation Service (TNS) established
      at Gravesend
1960   Diesel replaces steam on dock railways
1960   No. 4 berth and quay completed at
      Royal Victoria Dock
1962   Rochdale Report on UK ports issued
1963   Dartford tunnel opened
1963   First major consignment of packaged timber
      discharged in London
1964   Dudley Perkins appointed General Manager
1964   PLA sets up network of weather stations along
      the Thames
1964   Seaward boundary of PLA area of responsibility
      extended by 22 miles to its current limits
1965   Standard size of shipping containers fixed
1966   Devlin report on dock labour issued
1966   First voluntary severance scheme for dockers
1966   National seamen's strike

1966   Shipping Control Centre established
1966   Specialist packaged timber berth, No. 34, opened
      in Tilbury
1967   Complete decasualisation of dock labour achieved
1967   East India Export Dock closed
1967   Knock John Channel opened
1968   Bulk wine berth opened in Millwall Docks
1968   First transatlantic container ship arrives in Tilbury
1968   London and St Katharine Docks closed
1969   Bulk grain terminal opened at Tilbury
1969   First General Directions for the river issued
1969   New terminal for Fred Olsen opened in
      Millwall Docks
1970   New rail terminal opened at Tilbury
1970   Surrey Commercial Docks closed
1971   John Lunch appointed Director-General
1971   PLA divided for first time into business divisions:
      Upper Docks, Tilbury Docks and Grain Terminal,
      and Marine Services
1971   Trinity Square Head Office sold
1972   National dock strike
1973   Abolition of Temporarily Unattached Register
1973   PLA employed 8,925 people
1973   PLA takes over first stevedoring firm, Thames
      Stevedoring and Metropolitan Terminals
1973   Rebuilt London Bridge opened
1974   PLA takes over Gee Stevedoring
1974   PLA transfers responsibility for monitoring river
      pollution to Thames Water
1974   PLA transfers river piers to GLC
1975   *London Mammoth* sold
1975   PLA takes over Scruttons (stevedores)
1976   William Bowey appointed Managing Director
1977   John Black appointed Managing Director
1978   Cutler Street warehouses sold
1978   Government grants to fund severance payments
      first made to PLA
1978   Northfleet Hope container terminal opened
      at Tilbury
1979   PLA sole employer of stevedores in the Port
1980   PLA employed 6,670 people
1980   Second Dartford crossing opened

1980   West India and Millwall Docks closed

1981   London Docklands Development Corporation established

1981   Royal Docks closed

1982   Thames Flood Barrier completed

1984   Port of London Properties formed

1984   Port of London River Information System (POLARIS) introduced

1985   Tilbury passenger terminal renamed London International Cruise Terminal

1985   Vessel Traffic Services (VTS) – an improved TNS – becomes operational

1986   John Black retired as Chief Executive; PLA split into three divisions

1986   Last of surplus dockers leaves the PLA

1988   PLA became a competent harbour authority, assuming responsibility for pilotage on the tidal Thames

1989   PLA re-assumes responsibility for river piers

1989   National Dock Labour Scheme abolished

1989   Accident involving *Marchioness* pleasure boat and dredger *Bowbelle*

1990   Denton Wharf acquired

1990   Port Control Centre, including VTS, established at Gravesend

1991   Ilford Sports and Social Club closed

1991   PLA employed 1,408 people

1991   Queen Elizabeth II Bridge opened

1992   Port of Tilbury privatised

1992   PLA employed 464 people

1992   London River House, Gravesend, completed

1993   David Jeffery appointed PLA Chief Executive, having been Chief Executive, River Division

1993   Port Control Centre upgraded to handle vessels' GPS data

1993   Heaviest salmon caught by rod and line in the Thames for 160 years

1993   Thames Oil Spill Clearance Association (TOSCA) formed

1993   TNS and Pilotage Service amalgamated into Port Service London

1993   PLA takes over responsibility for navigation lights and buoys from Trinity House

1994   Financial agreement reached between PLA and the government

1995   Tilbury sold to Forth Ports

1997   PLA hosts 20th Biennial Conference of International Association of Ports and Harbors

1998   Shell Haven oil refinery closure announced

1998   Thames Clean joined with PLA driftwood operation to form Thames21

1998   VTS upgraded to Sofrelog Traffic Image Display System

1999   Shell Haven oil refinery closed

1999   PLA transfers five central London piers to London River Services

1999   Steve Cuthbert appointed Chief Executive

1999   Findings of the Thames Safety Inquiry reported

2000   Marchioness Formal Investigation took place

2000   Alexandra House, Gravesend, acquired

2000   Millennium Bridge opened

2000   Safety Management System (SMS) becomes operational

2003   Rebuilding of Denton Wharf quays and provision of a boat lift completed

2004   Richard Everitt appointed Chief Executive

2004   VTS upgraded to include AIS technology

2006   Marine House, Denton Wharf, completed

2007   Secretary of State supports planning inspector's recommendation on Peruvian Wharf

2007   PLA publishes first Environmental Report

2007   Secretary of State for Transport approves DP World's London Gateway container terminal project

2008   Deepening of Princes Channel completed

2008   PLA employment running at 360 people

2009   Port of London Authority celebrates one hundred years of service

TOTAL TONNAGE OF CARGOES PASSING THROUGH THE PORT OF LONDON

Year	(m tonnes)	Year	(m tonnes)	Year	(m tonnes)
1840	2	1936	41.6	1975	45.6
1850	3	1937	43.6	1976	48.6
1860	4.1	1938	45.3	1977	51
1870	5.1	1939	42.4	1978	49.5
1880	7.1	1940-46	na	1979	48.6
1890	10.1	1947	na	1980	48.1
1900	16.3	1948	37	1981	44
1910	18.9	1949	39.5	1982	41.6
1911	20	1950	41.3	1983	41.7
1912	19	1951	45.7	1984	43.2
1913	20.4	1952	50	1985	46.5
1914	19.1	1953	49.1	1986	48.3
1915	16	1954	52.2	1987	43.8
1916	12.9	1955	52.9	1988	48.9
1917	9.6	1956	54.8	1989	50.2
1918	7.9	1957	56.1	1990	54
1919	13.8	1958	56.4	1991	49.5
1920	16.8	1959	52.8	1992	44.5
1921	17.7	1960	58	1993	46
1922	20.1	1961	59.9	1994	47.4
1923	na	1962	58	1995	51.3
1924	21	1963	59.3	1996	52.7
1925	23.1	1964	62.3	1997	55.7
1926	24	1965	60.1	1998	56.4
1927	25	1966	60.3	1999	52.4
1928	na	1967	61.1	2000	47.9
1929	na	1968	62	2001	50.7
1930	36.7	1969	59	2002	51.2
1931	35.8	1970	60.4	2003	51
1932	34.5	1971	57.4	2004	53.3
1933	34.9	1972	54	2005	53.8
1934	37.3	1973	57.2	2006	51.9
1935	39.9	1974	51.5	2007	52.7

Notes:
The figures for 1840–1890 are estimated figures

There are no figures available for the Second World War

There are no figures available for 1923, 1928, 1929 or 1947

Source:
PLA box file on statistics held by the Museum in Docklands; PLA Annual Reports

CHAIRMEN OF THE PORT OF LONDON AUTHORITY

	Term of Office
Viscount Devonport	1909–1925
Lord Ritchie	1925–1941
Thomas Wiles	1941–1946
Viscount Waverley	1946–1958
Viscount Simon	1958–1970
Lord Aldington	1970–1977
Sir John Cuckney	1977–1979
Victor Paige	1980–1984
Sir Brian Kellett	1984–1992
Sir Brian Shaw	1993–2000
Simon Sherrard	2001–2009

NOTES ON SOURCES AND IMAGES

The literature on the Thames is almost infinite and the Port of London Authority archive is vast. I have concentrated on a limited number of sources and these are given below. I cannot thank Claire Frankland, Archivist, Port and River, at the Museum in Docklands, enough for all the help she gave me.

The PLA also has a large collection of images, the older images housed at the Museum in Docklands, the more recent at the PLA base in Gravesend. Claire Frankland and her colleague, Anna Sparham, Curator, Images, Later Department, Museum of London, were once again very generous with their time and advice in relation to the older images. The more recent images, many of them taken by Samuel Ashfield, were collated by Samantha Broome and her colleagues at the PLA. Where the copyright of older images was held outside the PLA, application was made to the identifiable copyright holders for permission to reproduce, and acknowledgement has been given in all such cases, including those where the copyright holder did not respond.

The key archival sources used were:

PLA Annual Report and Accounts
PLA Monthly
PLA Monthly Staff Supplements

Museum in Docklands, Oral History Collection

All images in the book are taken from either the PLA Collection held by the Museum in Docklands or the PLA's own current collection, unless otherwise stated.

The main secondary sources used were:

Ackroyd, Peter, *Thames – Sacred River*, London, 2007
Bates, L M, *The Thames on Fire – The Battle of London River 1939–1945*, Lavenham, 1985
Bates, L M, *Thames Cavalcade – The Heyday of the Haven*, Lavenham, 1991
Bentley, J, *East of the City – The London Docklands Story*, London, 1997
Bloomberg, J, *Looking Back – A Docker's Life*, London, 1979
Broodbank, Sir Joseph, *History of the Port of London*, 2 vols, London, 1921
Brown, R D, *The Port of London*, Lavenham, 1978
Clegg, W P, *Docks & Ports*, London, 1986
Croad, S, *Liquid History – The Thames Through Time*, London, 2003
Dash, J, *Good Morning, Brothers!*, London, 1969
Davies, S et al (eds), *Dock Workers*, Vol 1, Aldershot, 2000
Devonport, Viscount, *The Travelled Road, Some Memories of a Busy Life*, privately printed, nd
Ellmers, C, and Werner, A, *Dockland Life – A Pictorial History of London's Docks, 1860–2000*, London, 2000
Hardwicke, G, *Keepers of the Door – The History of the Port of London Police*, nd
Jackson, G, *The History & Archaeology of Ports*, Tadworth, 1983
Jamieson, A G, *Ebb Tide in the Marine Industries – Change & Adaptation 1918–1990*, Exeter, 2003
McLean, Rita, *The Downstream Dock – Tilbury 1886–1986*, Thurrock, 1986
Pudney, J, *London's Docks*, London, 1975
Oram, R B, *The Dockers' Tragedy*, London, 1975
Schneer, J, *The Thames – England's River*, London, 2005
Schweitzer, P, and Wegner, C (eds), *On the River – Memories of a Working River*, London, 1989
Tull, G J D, *The Port of London Authority 1909–1959*, PLA, 1959

CITY of LONDON

The Monument

Bakers Hall

The Hung, Drawn & Quartered P.H.

TOWER HILL

L o w e r   T h a m e s   S t r e e t

Custom House Wharf 141-2

Old Billingsgate Market

Custom House

145

Custom House Lower Stairs

Batavier Wharf

Three Quays

Tower Pier

Dark House Walk

143 Old Billingsgate Walk

Custom House Walk

146

Sugar Quay Walk

147

Wool Quays

Three Quays Walk

148

149

Tower Stairs

The Queen's Stairs

outfall

149a

Thames Leisure

Britton's Collar Barge

2PLA St. Botolph

PLA Tower Stairs

PLA Tower Bridge Upper

PLA Tower Bridge Upper

H.M.S. BELFAST 157

Tide gauge

Stairs

London Bridge City Pier

London Bridge Hospital

162 163

Cottons Centre

161

164

Livett's Launches

Dn

Dn

Marine Services

The Horniman P.H.

165

Hays Galleria

PLA Utility

Southwark Crown Court

166

170-174

The Queen's Walk

outfall

outfall

Utilities Tunnel

TOOLEY STREET

Cottons Lane

Hays Lane

Battlebridge Lane

Morgans Lane

City Hall

The Queen's Walk

London Bridge City Pa

175

Potters Fields